BUILT FOR THE AGES:

A History of the Grove Park Inn

by

Bruce E. Johnson

Published by The Grove Park Inn and Country Club

For additional copies of this book contact:

> The Grove Park Inn and Country Club
> 290 Macon Avenue
> Asheville, North Carolina 28804

Printed by Taylor Publishing Company
Dallas, Texas

Design by Jan Jones Pulley

Edited by Winston Fitzpatrick
>   Patricia Miller
>   Maggie Schlubach

Color photography by John Warner

Library of Congress Catalog Card Number: 91-71524

TABLE OF CONTENTS

ACKNOWLEDGMENTS

When I first stepped into the Great Hall at the Grove Park Inn, I had an overwhelming desire never to leave. Like thousands before me, I felt secure being surrounded by her massive granite walls, sturdy oak furniture, and proud, efficient staff. Over the course of the next five years, as I returned countless times, that feeling never diminished. As I learned more about Edwin W. Grove, Fred L. Seely, and the scores of individuals who had each left their mark on this historic hotel, I felt a need to add my own.

I owe a debt of gratitude to hundreds of people, only a few of whom I am able to thank here today. At the top of my list is the entire staff at the Grove Park Inn. Every individual at the inn was willing to stop at any time to answer my questions, to dig deep into their memories, and to share with me their experiences, for they, too, have been touched by this grand old hotel. Three individuals in particular have dedicated themselves to preserving the history of the Grove Park Inn. Without the efforts of Jane Rowe, Patricia Miller, and Maggie Schlubach, much of what we know about the Grove Park Inn today would have disappeared long ago. In addition, I would also like to thank my publishing consultant Susan McDonald, former general manager Herman von Treskow and owner Elaine D. Sammons, who approved, encouraged, and supported this important project.

A few of the many individuals who contributed information to this history include the Asheville *Citizen-Times* staff, the Biltmore Industries staff, Cynthia Bland, Gertrude Grove Bland, Harry Blomberg, Robert Bunn, Ted Carter, Adella Dilley, Frank and JoAnn Edwinn, David Erskine, Jane Gianvito, Robert Griffin, Robert Hitpas, Fred Kahn, Bill Kelley, Ed Leach, Rich Mathews, Richard Maxwell, Gwyn Bellamy McNutt, Mary Ashley Morris, Bill and Mildred Neilson, the Pack Memorial Library staff, S. M. Patton, Norman and Peggy Payne, Lilian Pierce, Wilda Robinson, Fred L. Seely, Jr., the Southern Highland Research Center, Lorraine Wilson, and many citizens of Paris, Tennessee; St. Louis, Missouri; and, of course, Asheville. I only regret that I did not have the time nor the space to interview the hundreds more who could have contributed to this book. I sincerely hope that their information, letters, and memories can be preserved within the Grove Park Inn archives for the next volume.

Finally, I would like to thank my wife, Dr. Lydia M. Jeffries, who endured with only an occasional complaint innumerable hours of G.P.I. trivia, and who continues to be my toughest critic, my strongest supporter, and my best friend.

Bruce E. Johnson

May 1, 1991

After a long mountain walk one evening, at the sunset hour, scarcely more than a year ago, I sat down here to rest, and while almost entranced by the panorama of these encircling mountains and a restful outlook upon green fields, the dream of an old-time inn came to me — an inn whose exterior, and interior as well, should present a home-like and wholesome simplicity, whose hospitable doors should ever be open wide, inviting the traveler to rest awhile, shut in from the busy world outside.

Edwin W. Grove
July 12, 1913

DESIGN AND CONSTRUCTION:
1912-1913

Edwin Wiley Grove, often called "the Father of Modern Asheville," was born on a small plantation near Bolivar, Tennessee, on December 23, 1850, the son of James and Elizabeth Grove. During the Civil War, Elizabeth Grove and her young son worked the family farm, while James Grove fought on the side of the Confederate army. After his father's return, young Edwin struck out on his own, possibly to Arkansas, where he may have studied pharmacy. In 1874, Edwin Grove arrived in Paris, Tennessee, where he became a clerk and pharmacist in a drug store owned by two of the town's most prominent citizens, Dr. Samuel H. Caldwell, a Civil War battlefield surgeon, and A.B. Mitchum, a local banker.

Workmen at the Grove Park Inn pause at the end of a spring day in 1913 for a photograph on the Sunset Terrace.

From the first days of his clerkship, Edwin Grove was determined not only to have his own business, but to discover a formula, a new compound, perhaps, that would set him apart from all other pharmacists. In a matter of months young Grove had persuaded the aging Dr. Caldwell and his partner to sell him their business, which he promptly renamed Grove's Pharmacy. "I had a little retail drug business in Paris, Tennessee," he later recalled, "just barely making a living, when I got up a real invention, tasteless quinine. As a poor man and a poor boy, I conceived the idea that whoever could produce a tasteless chill tonic, his fortune was made."

During the time Edwin Grove lived and worked, malaria stalked the South, killing thousands of men, women and children in devastating outbreaks that left thousands more too weak to work. Indian tribes in the Andes Mountains of South America had known for centuries that chewing the bark of the "fever tree" could ward off the deadly disease, but it was not until 1820 that scientists in Europe and America confirmed that quinine powder, refined from the bark of the cinchona tree, was an effective, though bitter-tasting, remedy for malaria.

As a Southern pharmacist, Edwin Grove was well aware of the deadly swath that malaria cut through the wetlands; he was equally aware of people's resistance to the quinine powder, the distasteful, but only known remedy for the disease. By 1878, only four years after he had arrived in Paris, Edwin Grove had developed his first formula for suspending quinine in a liquid and making it relatively tasteless. Grove named his original compound *Feberlin*, but because of its high level of quinine, it could only be sold by prescription. Grove continued to experiment with his formula until he discovered that he could reduce and disguise the bitter taste of quinine by adding iron, with sugar and lemon flavorings. The resulting nonprescription remedy, *Grove's Tasteless Chill Tonic*, proved to be an overnight sensation.

Regardless of its taste or form, quinine could not cure malaria. Once in the bloodstream, quinine would hinder the growth of the malarial parasite, reducing the patient's fever and chills, but could not destroy the actual parasite. To prevent a reccurence, the patient was advised by Grove to take four tablespoons daily of *Grove's Tasteless Chill Tonic* "for a period of eight weeks or during the entire malarial season." Considering the deadly threat posed by malaria, the ability of quinine to control, though not destroy, the parasite, and Grove's "tasteless" formula, it was little wonder that Grove's Pharmacy and his newly formed Paris Medicine Company soon outgrew their Tennessee home. In 1891 Grove moved his business north to St. Louis, where a more sophisticated railway system, a larger manufacturing facility, and a growing sales force soon made *Grove's Tasteless Chill Tonic* a household staple. Even decades later, long after the threat of malaria had been reduced, Grove's tonic remained popular, for it was widely advertised that it "restores Energy and Vitality by creating new, healthy blood." According to one source, more bottles of *Grove's Tasteless Chill Tonic* were sold in the late 1890s than were bottles of another recent Southern invention, Coca-Cola. And at a time when a typical factory worker might earn ten dollars a week, Edwin W. Grove, at the age of forty-four, became a millionaire.

Edwin W. Grove (1850-1927) was a familiar face to many Asheville residents. The famous inventor of Grove's Tasteless Chill Tonic spent the greater part of his summers after 1900 in the mountain city.

While Grove apparently had the Midas touch for the pharmaceutical business, his personal life was not as blessed. His young wife, Mary Louisa Moore Grove, died in 1884 while they lived in Paris; of their four children, only Evelyn, born in 1877, survived infancy. Two years later Grove married twenty-two year old Alice Gertrude Mathewson; a son, Edwin W. Grove, Jr., was born in 1890, but his third child, a daughter, died at an early age of diphtheria after the family had moved to St. Louis.

Though his financial future seemed secure, Edwin Grove continued to develop new pharmaceutical compounds, several of which were variations of his famous *Grove's Tasteless Chill Tonic* formula. At a time when most medicines came in either a liquid or powder form, he struck upon the idea to develop the first cold tablet, called *Grove's Laxative Bromo Quinine.* He first commissioned the fledgling Parke-Davis Company in Detroit to produce the tablets. While in Detroit to resolve a problem with his quinine tablets, Grove was introduced to one of Parke-Davis's most promising young managers, a man by the name of Fred Seely, who would soon become Grove's son-in-law.

The famous Grove trademark was the face of a baby, which in this advertisement was placed on the body of a plump pig. The slogan 'No Cure, No Pay' amounted to a money-back guarantee.

Fred Loring Seely was born in Monmouth, New Jersey, on December 22, 1871, the son of Uriah and Nancy Hopping Seely. He left school after the eighth grade, when his father secured for the thirteen-year-old Seely a position as an office boy with a New York City pharmaceutical firm. Seely later attended the New York College of Pharmacy and worked as a clerk for Johnson & Johnson in New York City before moving to Detroit to work for the Parke-Davis Company. He distinguished himself at Parke-Davis by inventing a machine to compress tablets. When the twenty-five-year-old Seely met Edwin Grove around 1896 — and subsequently solved Grove's problem with his quinine tablets — Seely had already risen to head the entire tablet manufacturing division of Parke-Davis.

In the early fall of 1913, William Jennings Bryan and his wife (rear, left) traveled to Asheville to visit the Seelys. Seated in the middle of the rear of the car is Evelyn Grove Seely. The woman on the right has tentatively been identified as Mrs. William Butt-Cody of Atlanta. The driver of the 1913 Packard is Fred L. Seely.

Grove was impressed with Fred Seely's determination, leadership, and innovative flair, especially in the new field of tablet manufacturing. He undoubtedly saw something of himself in the young man as well. Grove was forty-seven at the time; over the course of a hectic twenty years he had transformed a small-town drug store into a multimillion-dollar corporation, but it had taken its toll, as he had developed chronic insomnia and bronchitis. It appears, too, that Grove had begun to explore interests outside of the pharmaceutical world and may well have been looking for someone to take over the day-to-day operation of the Paris Medicine Company. Since his only son was just seven years old, Grove may have envisioned Fred Seely as his heir apparent. In any event, Edwin W. Grove soon introduced Fred L. Seely to his only daughter, Evelyn, and on October 24, 1898, the two were married in St. Louis.

Seely first met his future wife at Grove's residence in Asheville, where the Grove family had begun spending their summers on Grove's doctor's advice. In addition to suffering from chronic insomnia and occasional bouts with bronchitis, Grove also endured prolonged attacks of hiccoughs, some of which would last several months. Doctors in St. Louis suggested a vacation in Asheville, where he might meet a physician in one of the many tuberculosis sanitariums in the mountain community who could cure him of his malady. Though the attacks continued to plague him for the remainder of his life, Grove enjoyed the panoramic views of the Blue Ridge Mountains and the soothing climate, which also provided an escape from the stifling summer heat of St. Louis. In 1898 Grove decided to establish a residence in Asheville, as well as a branch of the Paris Medicine Company. That year Grove formed The Tasteless Quinine Company in Asheville and offered his new son-in-law the opportunity to manage it. Fred Seely accepted, but only remained in Asheville from 1898 until 1901, as Grove soon realized that Seely's wide range of skills would be better utilized at the main plant in St. Louis. Once Fred Seely had left Asheville, Grove dissolved The Tasteless Quinine Company, but he never lost interest in the city. In 1902 he, his wife, Gertrude, and their son Edwin W. Grove, Jr., moved into a magnificent new home at the corner of Liberty and Broad Streets; the knoll on which their home was built overlooked the undeveloped northern valley and Sunset Mountain.

In October of 1900, Edwin Grove sent his new son-in-law and his daughter on a five-month around-the-world cruise in search of new sources of quinine. The combination of increased competition and a dwindling supply of the slow-growing cinchona tree threatened the future of the Paris Medicine Company. Fred and Evelyn Seely boarded a steamer for the island of Java, the only location in the world where the cinchona trees were grown commercially; in his journal Seely later noted, "I think we felt nothing short of lonesome. 14,000 miles from home. Evelyn was the only American woman in Java and I believe there were 6 or 7 men in the Island who had been Americans at some time in their lives." Despite many setbacks, Seely negotiated a contract that secured for the Paris Medicine Company a steady supply of quinine for the next forty-two years.

In 1901 Fred L. Seely returned to St. Louis and reorganized the entire Paris Medicine Company, from the stenographic and bookkeeping departments to the advertising and manufacturing divisions. Sales of nearly every Grove product, whose numbers continued to grow, rose dramatically under his direction. Drawing upon his experience at Parke-Davis, Fred Seely invented a machine that would form, count, and box quinine tablets, which Edwin Grove had earlier foreseen as the first nonliquid cold medicine. Seely's invention not only enabled the Paris Medicine Company to become a world leader in the production and distribution of the popular cold tablets, it helped avert financial ruin as the threat of malaria receded. By 1905, however, it had become apparent that both Edwin Grove and Fred Seely were ready to seek new challenges beyond the world of pharmaceutical drugs. Grove had begun investing heavily in land in North Carolina, Georgia, Arkansas, and Florida, and started a residential subdivision, Fortified Hills, outside of Atlanta. Seely assisted Grove in marketing lots in Fortified Hills, but in 1905 they embarked on an even greater undertaking: the founding of a daily newspaper.

The Atlanta *Georgian* first appeared in 1906 with Fred L. Seely as its publisher and Edwin W. Grove as its principal stockholder. Through the efforts of Fred Seely, the Atlanta *Georgian* succeeded where other newspaper ventures had failed. His strong-willed editorials successfully fought to abolish chain-gang labor; he was an early and vigorous champion of Prohibition, and he both supported and participated in the 1912 Presidential campaign of New Jersey governor Woodrow Wilson. That same year, however, Grove and Seely sold the Atlanta *Georgian*, reportedly for a sizable profit, to newspaper magnate William Randolph Hearst.

By 1912, Edwin Grove was spending as much time on his real estate projects as he was on the management of the highly successful and quite profitable Paris Medicine Company. He had begun buying tracts of land in Asheville as early as 1902; much of the land he first purchased was timberland, but after the success of Fortified Hills in Atlanta he decided to develop lots on Sunset Mountain on the north edge of Asheville. Grove had watched as the publicity generated by George Vanderbilt's palatial summer home, Biltmore Estate, completed in 1895, as well as the subsequent expansion of the Southern Railway system, had spurred interest in Asheville. A few years after establishing a summer residence in Asheville, Grove was prepared to take part in the growth of the city and to reap the benefits from his involvement. In 1904, even before selling his first lot, he established the E. W. Grove Park near the north end of Charlotte Street and, just as he had done in Fortified Hills, named the new streets of his adjacent development for members of his family.

The E. W. Grove Park Company, with headquarters in a one-story office still standing in Grove Park, faced stiff competition from real estate developers selling residential lots in the village of Biltmore Forest two miles south of Asheville. Incorporation papers filed for his company in 1912 declared that, in addition to buying, selling, and developing land for residential real estate, the stockholders also intended "to own, build, erect, construct, manage, and occupy buildings for hotel purposes" and "to quarry, mine, cut, saw, finish, set, purchase, sell and deal in marble or other stone." Of the shares originally issued by the new corporation, E. W. Grove of St. Louis held 998. The remaining were issued to W. F. Randolph, his real estate manager in Asheville, and John S. Adams, a local attorney.

Grove and Randolph first discussed the idea of a resort hotel on the western slope of Sunset Mountain as early as 1909, but since Asheville, with a population of approximately 18,000, was better known for its tuberculosis sanitariums than its tourist attractions, Grove was hesitant. The social life of the city revolved around its most popular landmark — the Battery Park Hotel. Although Grove owned most of the land on and below Sunset Mountain, in 1910 it was occupied by more cows than houses. With encouragement from prominent townspeople and the Southern Railway, Grove gave W.F. Randolph permission to solicit architectural sketches for a new hotel. In their many letters, Grove and Randolph analyzed structural elements in nearly a dozen hotels across the country, but it was not until Grove's secretary gave him a brochure entitled "The Hotels of Yellowstone Park" that they discovered the type of resort they wanted to build. On November 6, 1911, Randolph wrote to Grove, "We have the photographs and interiors sent by Mrs. Williams and regard them as the finest we have seen. We are glad to have material of this kind in view of the similar development you propose here."

Despite having photographs of the Old Faithful Inn and the Grand Canyon Hotel to show prospective architects, none were able to design a hotel that met Grove's expectations. Beginning February 26, 1912, each of the architects, including Asheville's own firm of Smith and Carrier, received the following notice: "The various hotel plans submitted do not meet with Mr. Grove's approval; he is not desirous of continuing the competition." From his newspaper office in Atlanta, Fred Seely had begun to correspond in 1911 with Robert G. Reamer, the architect of the Old Faithful Inn. Then, in May, Seely presented Grove with a sketch he had made of the proposed inn. A letter written by Fred Seely to a friend the following month explains what had happened: "We did not succeed in getting a satisfactory plan from any of the architects and for that reason I undertook it myself and, strangely, made a plan that suited Mr. Grove." Seely's sketch, a photograph of which has survived, reveals his debt to the Old Faithful Inn, but rather than constructing the inn of logs, as Grove had envisioned, Seely suggested using native boulders from Grove's surrounding land.

Although he had no previous experience, Fred L. Seely submitted this sketch of the proposed hotel to Edwin W. Grove in May of 1912. Little more than a year later, the completed inn varied only slightly from Seely's first drawing.

The only piece of motorized equipment used to carve a ledge on Sunset Mountain was a single steamshovel, used to fill a steady stream of two-wheeled carts pulled by mules. The golf course and Kimberly Avenue can be seen in the background.

With a plan in hand, Grove acted quickly. He and Randolph had carefully selected a site for the Grove Park Inn from the hundreds of acres in Grove's vast holdings. Located nearly 2500 feet above sea level, it would provide guests with a panoramic view of Asheville and the western rim of the Blue Ridge Mountains, yet, unlike a proposed site at the top of the mountain, would not put them at the mercy of the elements. Grove accurately calculated that being adjacent to the Asheville Country Club and one of the finest eighteen-hole golf courses in the South would only increase the attractiveness of his hotel. In May of 1912, Edwin W. Grove and Fred L. Seely walked the slope of Sunset Mountain and talked about their vision of the Grove Park Inn. As Seely later wrote, "The idea was to build a big home where every modern convenience could be had, but with all the old-fashioned qualities of genuineness with no sham... all attempt at the bizarre, the tawdry and flashily foolish [would be] omitted."

Hundreds of mules pulled wagons and sleds full of rocks and boulders down from the mountain to the road where the "automobile train" waited.

The famous Grove "automobile train" was led by one of his three Packard trucks pulling fifteen wagons of rocks containing more than forty tons of boulders.

By mid-June, Seely and Grove had selected J. W. McKibben of Atlanta as the hotel's architectural engineer and J. Oscar Mills, also of Atlanta, as the construction superintendent. Both men had worked for Grove on the Fortified Hills subdivision in Atlanta. Seely, McKibben, and Mills spent the month of June developing the plan for the hotel. While Fred Seely provided the overall design, J.W. McKibben, a certified architect, translated Seely's and Grove's ideas into detailed blueprints for Oscar Mills to follow. Groundbreaking took place on July 9, 1912, with Edwin Grove's wife, Gertrude, turning the first shovelful of dirt. According to the *Asheville Citizen,* "the plans were worked out by F. L. Seely, who has recently moved here for perma-

nent residence. Mr. Seely's plans follow the simple but strong lines of a period in English architecture that builded for homely comforts."

Fred Seely and Edwin Grove had decided it was imperative that the inn be open for the following summer season; they announced to reporters present at the groundbreaking that the scheduled date of completion would be July 1, 1913. From his wooden office perched on the construction site, Oscar Mills immediately began hiring a crew of about four hundred men of various ages and races. Grove's wages were the best in the area: one dollar a day for a ten-hour shift. Many of his workers had walked away from other projects to work on the hotel; Grove

A young boy was kept busy supplying water to the men widening the road leading to the Grove Park Inn.

While the stonemasons work above them, workmen prepare to pour the concrete floor for the inn's dining room. The workman in the center is standing where the north fireplace would later rise. Note the scaffolding, ramps, and forms utilized in the construction of the inn.

J. Oscar Mills, who had worked for Edwin W. Grove on a construction project in Atlanta, came to Ashevillle to serve as construction superintendent under Fred Seely. In the summer of 1912, he and his family posed on the first pile of rocks brought to the site.

reportedly also brought scores of laborers from the deep South and erected a huge circus tent to temporarily house them. Aided only by a solitary steamshovel and scores of mules, the men set to work leveling the site, hauling countless tons of stone from Grove's surrounding properties, and constructing wooden scaffolding, undoubtedly supplied by Grove's sawmill and lumberyard in nearby Madison County.

Using mules, pullies, and ropes, the men collected granite stones, some weighing as much as ten thousand pounds, from land on several nearby mountains, including Sunset, Beaucatcher, and Black Mountains. Teams of mules dragged the boulders onto wooden sleds and pulled them down to the road. The stones were then hoisted into wagons supplied by a local Asheville business, T. S. Morrison & Co. Approximately fourteen wagons were strung together to form a train pulled to the site by one of three Packard trucks Grove owned. This unique "automobile train" could haul forty tons of rock per trip and was featured in several national publications.

Asheville photographer John Robinson crawled out onto the partially completed north wing on February 28, 1913, to capture carpenters building the forms for the concrete roof.

Each of the concrete roofs over the Main Inn were poured continuously to avoid any unnecessary seams. Large lights were installed to aid the men working at night on the roof.

Using one steamshovel and several mule-powered drags, workers at the site cut a long ledge into Sunset Mountain for the foundation of the six-story structure. Italian stonemasons, some of whom had worked on the Biltmore mansion twenty years earlier, followed Seely's instructions carefully, making sure that only the exposed, uncut side of each stone remained visible. As Seely later documented, "The men worked under instructions that when the Inn was finished not a piece of stone should be visible to the eye except it show the time-eaten face given to it by the thousands of years of sun and rain that had beaten upon it as it had lain on the mountain side. These great boulders were laid with the lichens and moss on them just as they were found."

Crates of red clay tile line the ramp leading to the south wing in the spring of 1913, as workmen weave a web of steel rod in preparation for the concrete roof.

As the stone walls rose, the carpenters constructed long wooden ramps for the men pushing wheelbarrows of rocks up to the stonemasons. Just six months after the groundbreaking, more than 1200 lineal feet of granite walls, some more than four feet thick at the base and six stories tall, were nearly complete. Workers began pouring the concrete floor in the lobby while the stonemasons were completing the walls above them; when the time came to pour the upper floors, a crude elevator designed to lift huge buckets of wet concrete rose through the center of the building.

Italian stonemasons, some of whom had worked on the Biltmore mansion, apply the stonework to the interior west wall of the Great Hall. The north fireplace would later be built in the area in the upper right of this photograph.

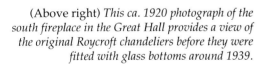
(Above left) *Chains, pulleys, and timbers were used to hoist the massive boulders into place. This photograph was taken during the construction of the north fireplace in the Great Hall.*

(Above right) *This ca. 1920 photograph of the south fireplace in the Great Hall provides a view of the original Roycroft chandeliers before they were fitted with glass bottoms around 1939.*

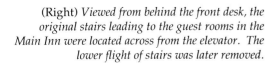
(Right) *Viewed from behind the front desk, the original stairs leading to the guest rooms in the Main Inn were located across from the elevator. The lower flight of stairs was later removed.*

By February, the construction foreman, J. Oscar Mills, was ready to start pouring the first of five individual roofs that would cover the inn. The highest, over the Great Hall, represented one of the largest continuous-pour concrete roofs of its day. Atop the wooden forms, the men first wove a steel web of half-inch reinforcing rods. The square, twisted steel rods, some thirty-five feet in length, intersected at six-inch intervals, horizontally as well as vertically. The steel rods added more than ninety thousand pounds of weight to the roof, supported by the massive granite walls and six concrete pillars extending through the main lobby and into the basement. Once the rods were in place, the men began pouring more than five inches of concrete over the forms in a continuous, round-the-clock operation. In a letter dated March 24, 1913, Mills wrote to his family in Georgia, "I had to come back to the hotel tonight. They are pouring the concrete roof on and are working sometimes all night. I came down off the roof and taken these few minutes to write You all; the wind is blowing up on the roof like fury. I can see all over Asheville, but Good Lord how one peep of Dear Old Atlanta would stir the latent blood in my veins."

Dated November 2, 1912, this photograph bears the caption **"The men who are building the Grove Park Inn, Asheville, N. C."** *Construction superintendent Oscar Mills can be seen in the back row, left of center, wearing a hat, gloves, and a buttoned overcoat.*

Once the concrete had cured, each of the roofs was sealed with five layers of hot asphalt and roofing felt. On top of the final layer the men laid red tile shingles, each approximately six inches wide, twelve inches long, and three-eighths of an inch thick, supplied by the Murray Roofing Company in Cloverport, Kentucky. To give the roof the desired English thatch-like appearance, the tiles were arranged in an irregular pattern around the dormers. As a reporter noted, "There will be no angles anywhere in the roof. There will be only lazy, graceful slopes and the effect will be something unique for this section of the country."

In March, as soon as the concrete roof was completed, workmen began finishing the interior. Plumbers attached water pipes for the guest rooms to the three-foot-square concrete pillars in the lobby, after which the stonemasons covered them with granite. At the ends of the 120-foot room rose the two massive fireplaces, inspired by the fireplace in Old Faithful Inn. According to an early brochure, each of the 36-foot-wide fireplaces required 120 tons of granite boulders to construct. The firebox in each is capable of burning twelve-foot logs atop the hammered iron andirons that "weigh five hundred pounds apiece, and an average of

twenty-four days' blacksmith work was done on each of them." A unique feature of the fireplaces is the way the elevators are concealed within them. Seely reportedly designed the elevators within the huge fireplaces to remove them from sight and to eliminate the noise they generated. He also housed the machinery in the basement, far away from guest rooms.

Several months prior to the inn's opening, Fred Seely had contacted his good friend, Elbert Hubbard, founder of the Roycroft Shops in East Aurora, N.Y., regarding furnishings. Having visited Hubbard at the Roycroft Inn, Seely was well aware of the high-quality furniture, lighting, and metalware produced in the Roycroft Shops, and offered him the opportunity to provide furnishings for the Grove Park Inn. Hubbard, in his characteristic style, immediately announced to the readers of his monthly magazine that "The Grove Park Inn could never be complete in its fulfillment of purpose without the assistance of The Roycrofters. And so it is that the dining room will be entirely furnished with Roycroft furniture — plain,

simple, straight-line pieces, genuinely handmade and with the quality the first and last endeavor. Too, from The Roycrofters' Copper Shop will come the lighting fixtures. These are also being made after special designs, with the loving marks of the hammer still on them. Nothing crude or impractical, but along the line of the most modern methods of illuminating, indirect lighting. Not an electric bulb will be seen."

The Roycroft craftsmen furnished for the opening banquet more than four hundred oak chairs, each bearing the Roycroft shopmark and the initials GPI carved into the crestrail. In addition, they constructed four large corner servers and two massive sideboards for the dining room, and a number of chairs, tables, and accessories for the offices, parlors, and billiard rooms, as well as the famous eight-foot-tall clock that originally greeted guests as they walked through the front doors. The Great Hall also featured large, comfortable wicker rocking chairs, straight chairs, and writing tables for the guests. The gray tile floor was covered with hand-made rugs imported from Aubusson, France, reportedly at a cost of more than five thousand dollars.

The rooms in the Main Inn were decorated with furniture by the White Furniture Company and lights by the Roycrofters. Many of the original furnishings are still in use today, although the footboards and burlap wallpaper have been removed.

The small Roycroft workshop in East Aurora was unable to provide, in the short amount of time allowed, the more than twelve hundred beds, dressers, tables, and chairs required for the 156 guest rooms surrounding the Palm Court. Upon learning this, J.S. White of the White Furniture Company in Mebane, North Carolina, contacted Fred Seely. As he later recalled, "Mr. Seely was a very exacting man and a hard worker and wanted everything perfect and did not believe that a furniture manufacturer in the South could make furniture satisfactory to them. After examining the sample, Mr. Seely was convinced that we could make the furniture, but had decided in the meantime that he wanted it made out of solid white oak and wanted to know if the samples could be delivered in ten days. We made the furniture and had it up there in ten days. It was absolutely satisfactory. Mr. Seely was so pleased with our work that he asked us to make many of the doors and other pieces used throughout the hotel."

Asheville photographer John G. Robinson (1880-1921) documented the construction of the inn with several dozen photographs, including this one taken in the original dining room.

The Roycrofters' Copper Shop, under the direction of Victor Toothaker, a well-known designer and artist, rose to the challenge of producing all the lighting for the Grove Park Inn. Each of the 156 guest rooms was outfitted with two, sometimes three, Roycroft table lamps, as well as a copper ceiling light suspended on iron chains. All of the hallways and various public rooms featured Roycroft ceiling lights, including eight copper and mica chandeliers in the original dining room and twelve in the spacious lobby. Seely also commissioned the Copper Shop to provide, in addition to the more than seven hundred lighting fixtures, approximately 2500 hammered-copper drawer pulls to be installed on the bedroom tables and dressers manufactured by the White Furniture Company.

As the July 1, 1913, deadline approached, it became apparent that the inn was not going to be ready on the appointed day. Photographs taken the last week in June reveal that neither the main tile roof nor the tile floor in the lobby was complete. A nearby stack of furniture intended for the bedrooms may have indicated that they, too, were not yet ready for guests. Invitations bearing a revised Fred Seely drawing depicting how the inn would appear after the landscaping had been completed were hastily prepared. Each one bore E. W. Grove's name and read, in part:

On the night of Saturday, July 12th, we expect to hold our opening banquet – opening the Grove Park Inn to the public.

We have built what we believe we can honestly claim is the finest resort hotel in the world, and on that night we shall be honored by the presence of the Secretary of State, William Jennings Bryan, who will make the principal address.

I believe it is generally known that this enterprise was not born of purely commercial motives, but was the outgrowth of a movement set on foot by Mayor Rankin and a number of prominent business men of this section who finally called on me at Saint Louis and placed the matter before me. After deciding to act upon their suggestion I did what I could to build an hotel worthy of these wonderful mountains.

I sincerely trust, therefore, that you may be present at seven p.m., Saturday, July 12th, to view the building before the banquet, which is to be at eight o'clock.

Four hundred of the most distinguished men of the South gathered on Saturday night, July 12, 1913, as Secretary of State William Jennings Bryan (not pictured) marked the official opening of the 156-room hotel by proclaiming it was "built for the ages." (S. H. Research Center)

A local newspaper reporter documented the opening ceremonies, noting that when the appointed hour arrived, "the four hundred guests were greeted by an army of gray-coated attendants. The great hostelry looked as if it had been completed for a year; not one person could realize that only two weeks ago chaos and disorder reigned on every side. While some portions of the hotel and the surrounding grounds have yet to receive the finishing touches, it stands today as it will stand for all time –

a marvel of the builder's art, a triumph of architectural skill. There was no confusion in the reception or in the allotment of guests, and the elaborate menu was served with perfect precision. Seldom has a more representative gathering assembled in this immediate section. With a cabinet officer, senators, and congressmen, men high in the various professions, men whose total wealth would run up into the millions, last night's gathering was an auspicious one in every way, and will be long remembered."

The eastern view of the inn appears today much as it did when this photograph was taken around 1920, revealing how well the soft roof line and granite boulders blend with the natural surroundings.

Fred Seely served as toastmaster at the elaborate, all-male dinner, after which he introduced each of the four speakers. Edwin W. Grove credited his son-in-law with the completion of the Grove Park Inn in twelve months' time: "A man never grows too old to build castles and dream dreams. Standing here tonight in the midst of my friends and invited guests, I find a dream realized and a castle materialized. It affords me far more gratification than I can express in having in my immediate family an architect and builder who, by his artistic conception, by his untiring zeal, has studied out the very minutest detail, making my dream a reality indeed and accomplishing what, in so short a time, seems almost beyond human endurance."

It remained for Secretary of State William Jennings Bryan to place the feat into historical perspective, as he observed: "Today we stand in this wonderful hotel, not built for a few, but for the multitudes that will come and go. I congratulate these men. They have built for the ages." Mayor Rankin, nearly overshadowed by the presence of Secretary of State Bryan, had nothing but praise for Edwin Grove:

By his brilliant fellowship, his broad enlightenment, and gracious hospitality, he has endeared himself to our population. In the great developments he has become a benefactor to Asheville. The successful completion of this handsome and magnificent structure not only now symbolizes the great public spirit of Dr. Grove, but it will be a monument to remind those who shall follow him of his foresight and accomplishment.

In the construction of the Grove Park Inn is to be found a natural beauty and art coupled with the ingenuity of man. This magnificent hotel typifies and embodies the acme of perfection in architectural design and is equipped with every convenience which lends to the comfort of its guests.

Here we see the triumph of architectural skill mingled with a scenic splendor of nature's handiwork, the whole blending in one great harmony never before equaled in the annals of the builders' craft.

Grove Park Inn
Asheville N.C.   Robinson

We are three and a half miles from the railroad. The street cars are not allowed to come near enough to be heard. Automobiles are not allowed near the building during the night. Thus we have no smoke, no dust, no train noise. We have pure air, common sense, digestible food, quiet in the bedrooms at night, the finest orchestra outside of New York and Boston, a great organ, and an atmosphere where refined people and busy business men with their families find great comfort and a good time.

Fred L. Seely

1920

THE AGE OF AUSTERITY: *1913-1927*

Although they were not permitted to smoke in the Great Hall, no one kept the ladies off the golf course. This photograph illustrates how the more than five hundred feet of open terrace nearly ringed the inn.

The Grove Park Inn's first guests were greeted by general manager William S. Kenney, formerly of the prestigious Mount Washington Hotel in Bretton Woods, New Hampshire. Most of the staff had been recruited from hotels from Miami to New York to Boston; one exception was the Grove Park Inn's first head of social affairs, Miss Gene Smith of Asheville. With Mr. Kenney in charge of the hotel's day-to-day operation, Edwin W. Grove turned his attention to plans for a new pharmaceutical factory in St. Louis. An ad that same year proclaimed that in 1912 the Paris Medicine Company had sold more than seven million boxes of *Grove's Laxative Bromo Quinine* tablets, now being touted as "The Original One Day Cold Cure."

Fred L. Seely, however, apparently had no intention of returning to St. Louis or to the Paris Medicine Company. His first few months away from the Grove Park Inn were undoubtedly spent at Overlook Castle, his spacious retreat atop Sunset Mountain on thirteen acres of land Grove had given him upon his arrival in Asheville. Construction of Overlook Castle, which Fred Seely and J. W. McKibbens had designed, had begun early in 1913, but would not be completed until 1919. The forty-two-year-old Seely seemed uncertain what career he might next undertake, for in a letter written just two days after the opening of the Grove Park Inn, William Jennings Bryan counseled him, "I have been thinking since I saw you of your future. You mentioned the

One of the first national advertisements for the Grove Park Inn appeared in the November 1913 issue of **National Geographic.** *This view was taken on the west terrace looking south, over the rows of famous rocking chairs.*

ministry. Each of us must at his peril interpret for himself the call to duty, but I have been wondering whether it might not be worth your while to consider the starting of a school. You have the executive ability and the zeal. Dr. Grove has both the spiritual incentive and the monies."

The assassination of Archduke Francis Ferdinand of Austria-Hungary on June 28, 1914, however, altered the course of millions of lives, including that of Fred L. Seely. World War I locked England, France, Russia, and eventually the United States in a deadly struggle with Germany and Austria-Hungary that would rob more than ten million men of their lives. Anticipating both America's involvement in the war and a crippling decline in business, Edwin W. Grove announced, late in the summer of 1914, his intent to close the Grove Park Inn until the war had ended. Despite his lack of experience in hotel management, Fred Seely was determined not to see the Grove Park Inn sit empty. Soon after Grove's unexpected announcement, Fred L. Seely offered to lease the Grove Park Inn from his father-in-law.

Grove Park Inn

Finest Resort Hotel in the World
Sunset Mountain
Asheville, N.C.

Absolutely Fireproof
Open all the Year

The Altitude
Makes it Cool in Summer

We do not entertain conventions. We have found that they disturb the homelike atmosphere of the Inn and interfere with the comfort of guests.

In 1920 Fred L. Seely published a fourteen-page booklet describing in great detail the Grove Park Inn. It was during this time that he also began including the "ghost wing," seen here on the far right; although he intended to build it, this wing never existed other than on re-touched photographs and postcards from this era.

1919 through 1927. If at any time the gross annual receipts at the Grove Park Inn were to exceed $300,000, Grove was to receive eight per cent of any revenues above that amount. Judging from the reductions in Grove's percentage, it would appear that business did decline during the war years, but Fred Seely's skill and determination kept the inn open and operating without interruption.

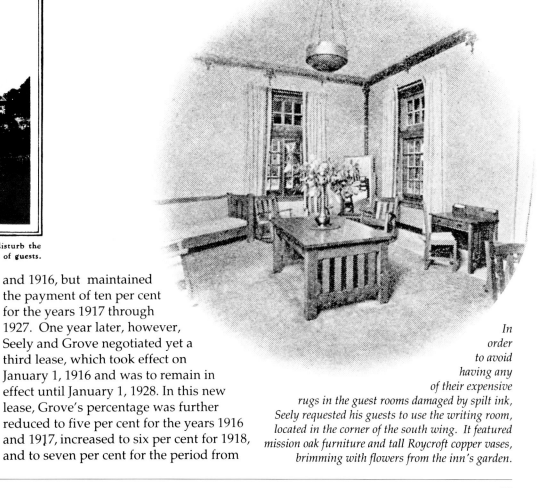

In order to avoid having any of their expensive rugs in the guest rooms damaged by spilt ink, Seely requested his guests to use the writing room, located in the corner of the south wing. It featured mission oak furniture and tall Roycroft copper vases, brimming with flowers from the inn's garden.

The term of the first lease Seely and Grove signed, in November of 1914, extended from January 1, 1915 until January 1, 1927. As first written, during the first two years Edwin W. Grove would receive eighteen per cent of all gross revenues and for the next ten years, ten per cent. This initial lease never took effect, but was renegotiated on December 9, 1914, and replaced by a lease which reduced Grove's percentage to eight per cent of the gross receipts for the years 1915 and 1916, but maintained the payment of ten per cent for the years 1917 through 1927. One year later, however, Seely and Grove negotiated yet a third lease, which took effect on January 1, 1916 and was to remain in effect until January 1, 1928. In this new lease, Grove's percentage was further reduced to five per cent for the years 1916 and 1917, increased to six per cent for 1918, and to seven per cent for the period from

Fine rugs imported from France provided a dash of color on the inn's original grey tile floor. The famous eight-foot-tall Roycroft clock can barely be seen against the second column from the right, where for decades it greeted guests coming through the front door.

In his customary style, Fred Seely set to work organizing, promoting, and managing the Grove Park Inn. From the first day of his reign it was apparent that the inn would reflect much of Fred Seely's personal philosophy. Alcohol was neither served nor permitted at the inn, even though Prohibition was still four years away. Although Seely was a nonsmoker, Roycroft oak and copper smoking stands were placed in the Great Hall, but, as a 1922 brochure stated, "Ladies are requested not to smoke in the public rooms. We do not make this request with any inclination to be critical. It is simply a rule that has been observed ever since the inn

was built and we believe that it conforms to the feelings of the majority of our household." Four ladies' parlors, as well as a writing room and management offices, were located on the first floor in the south wing. All were furnished with mission oak furniture, but the ladies' parlors also featured twenty-two-inch-tall copper Roycroft American Beauty vases designed to hold fresh flowers picked from the inn's gardens.

All guests in the Great Hall were expected to speak in hushed tones; those who were talking or laughing too loudly would be handed a printed card requesting that they be more subdued. At least one guest, Irwin Cobb, a well-known comedian, objected to this particular rule, for, upon being asked to lower his voice, Cobb sat quietly for a moment, then removed his shoes, and, in an exaggerated motion, tiptoed to the front desk, where, in hushed tones, he requested his bill.

Fred Seely was adamant in his belief that the men who patronized the Grove Park Inn expected peace and quiet. A 1918 *New York Times* ad proclaimed, "If you are a Big Business Man and feel the need of rest after these years of strain, you should come to the Grove Park Inn, Asheville, N.C. where rest is made possible." No automobiles were permitted to enter the grounds after 10:30 p.m. or before 9:00 a.m. Employees wearing rubber-heeled shoes reported to their hall stations at eight o'clock to be available if needed by the guests, but were instructed not to begin cleaning or making noise of any kind before nine. A sign in each elevator requested that guests not run water or make any unnecessary noise after 10:30 p.m. For a time, in fact, Seely in-

structed his employees to turn off the water to the guest rooms after 10:30 p.m. to ensure that no one would be disturbed by any running water. As Seely explained in one of his brochures, "We must insist upon protecting the rights of guests who may have retired, and as the Inn was located purposely away from railroads, street cars and other outside annoyances, conversations, slamming of doors, throwing shoes on the floor and similar unnecessary noises are liable to annoy guests in adjoining rooms.... We consider that our bedrooms are for rest after a reasonable hour, and we have the courage to enforce a discipline that makes rest possible."

(Following page) *The third floor Palm Court, illuminated by a skylight more than forty feet above it, has provided guests with a quiet retreat since its opening. It appears today much as it did when this photograph was taken in 1920.*
(S. H. Research Center)

(Above) *Fred Seely had the following notice printed on a window-shade, to be pulled down when appropiate in the elevator:*
"Please be quiet in going to your room – other guests may be asleep. No objections to remain in the Big Room as late as you like, but we greatly desire quiet in bedrooms and corridors from 10:30 p.m. to 8:00 a.m."

(Previous page) *Many of the guests at the hotel often came simply to relax on its open terraces amid its famous rocking chairs. These guests were captured in a ca. 1913 John Robinson photograph as they enjoyed the early morning sun on the east terrace.*

(Below) *The original forty-foot swimming pool located in the lower level of the inn was removed during the early thirties. This room later became a meeting room and is currently used as an employee training classroom.*

To that same end, Seely also discouraged guests from bringing small children to the Grove Park Inn. "We entertain very few children," he wrote. "Not that we dislike children, but that we wish to maintain a place where tired busy people may get away from excitement and all annoyances and rest their nerves." At the same time he also insisted that "Positively no dogs of any size, value, color or

ugliness [are] allowed at the Inn. Guests who attempt to smuggle them in in vanity boxes or suit cases will be asked to vacate their rooms. Sorry, but the Inn is for human beings who want to rest and recreate." Seely's efforts did not go unappreciated by his elite clientele. After spending six weeks at the Grove Park Inn in 1920, R. H. Borden, the Prime Minister of Canada, wrote to Fred Seely, "I have

A row of Roycroft "GPI" chairs lined the inn's three-lane bowling alley, located, until it was removed around 1930, in the room directly beneath the west terrace.

installed above the north fireplace, but, as he assured his guests, "We try always to secure plays and travel pictures and we take the trouble to censor every film carefully on a testing machine we have in a dark room in our general offices, before showing at our evening entertainment. This enables us to use many pictures that are excellent but would hardly be acceptable to us uncensored."

In 1919, Fred Seely purchased a Skinner organ, "the masterpiece of the greatest organ builder the world has ever produced," and had it installed in the southwest corner of the Great Hall. Ernest M. Skinner traveled by train from Boston to personally supervise the installation, which, according to a 1920 brochure,

twelve inches of solid concrete for absolute sound-proofing. Fred Seely also arranged for entertainment nearly every evening in the Great Hall, including string quartets, organists, vocalists, and lecturers. After each performance the staff would distribute Washington apples, along with a sheet of thin, grey paper for the core. When motion pictures grew popular, Seely had a large screen

more than once expressed to you my appreciation of the fine purpose which you have in mind in the management of the Grove Park Inn. No lesson is more necessary or more worthy than that which teaches the self-centered to remember reasonable consideration of others."

Despite the austere rules which he implemented, Fred Seely did make provisions for the entertainment, convenience, and recreation of his guests. He had designed into the lower level of the Grove Park Inn a forty-foot indoor swimming pool and adjacent shower rooms, a three-lane bowling alley, a billiards room, a game room, a pharmacy, and a barber shop (all of which were removed in later remodelings), but, as he pointed out, the ceiling above these rooms consisted of

For many years, guests at the inn could enjoy a game of billiards in the recreation room directly below the west terrace. The inn's three-lane bowling alley was located at the far end of this same room, since remodeled into accounting department offices.

Plush, red leather rockers added to the restful environment offered by the Grove Park Inn's Great Hall, first called the "Big Room." A sample of Fred Seely's mottoes can be seen on the rock walls and columns in this 1920 photograph.
(S. H. Research Center)

"required over sixty miles of wire for the electrical work. It requires a fifteen horse power motor to blow it and there are in the neighborhood of seven thousand pipes. It required three freight cars to bring it from the factory and four months to install it." For years afterward an organist provided guests with regular recitals, some of which were broadcast over a local radio station.

The menus at the Grove Park Inn reflected Fred Seely's concern for the selection and preparation of high-quality, healthful foods. Fresh seafood was brought directly from the coast; waiters served bread in the dining room from portable, heated warmers; and all the milk and cream came from the famous Biltmore Dairy on the Vanderbilt estate. Detailed descriptions of the source and means of

Arms were added to the original Roycroft dining chairs by woodworkers at Biltmore Industries prior to 1920. When this room was remodeled into staff offices in 1988, the original Roycroft lighting fixtures were transferred to the new Blue Ridge Dining Room. (S. H. Research Center)

Horse-drawn and horseless carriages were a familiar sight at the Grove Park Inn in its early years. Note the unused building stone piled near the open terrace on the east side of the building.

preparation of each course were included on every menu, including advice for guests with chronic gastric problems: "Nearly everyone should eat fruit of some kind, and most people want it for breakfast. We supply the finest prunes packed anywhere in the world — they are preserved at the orchards in California and are not the usual dried prune. We serve

them every morning year round." Guests planning to stay at the inn for an extended period would be assigned a particular table and waiter for each of their meals; beginning with the second morning of their stay, a copy of their hometown newspaper would be on their table at breakfast.

Both Grove and Seely took steps to prevent potential guests from avoiding the Grove Park Inn simply because of Asheville's long association with tuberculosis sanitariums. Grove, in his characteristic manner, purchased a number of tuberculosis sanitariums and boarding houses and tore them down; he also attached covenants to any lots which he sold preventing the building of any structures to be used to house or treat tuberculous patients. Seely stressed in his advertisements and brochures that the "Grove Park Inn is not a sanitarium, a hospital, or a health resort. It is a resting place for tired people who are not sick, who want good food well-cooked and

digestible, with luxurious, thorough sanitary surroundings." As a further precaution and assurance, the water at the inn, which, like all of Asheville's water, was piped seventeen miles from the slopes of Mt. Mitchell, was tested monthly and declared "as pure as nature ever produces." In addition, all silverware, glasses, and dishes were boiled not once, but twice, after each use. Even the coins used at the Grove Park Inn were washed in a special machine kept in the basement before being handed out to guests in change, and only crisp, new bills were issued to the front desk staff each morning.

*A few of the most famous guests to have stayed at the inn posed for this photograph in 1918. From left to right are Harvey Firestone, Sr.; Thomas A. Edison; Harvey Firestone, Jr., a man identified as Horatio Seymour, editor of the New York **World,** but who bears an uncanny resemblance to E. W. Grove; Henry Ford; and Fred Seely.*

A northwest view of the inn a few years after the opening shows many of the young pine trees which Seely had planted. Though many were destroyed in subsequent expansions, several examples still survive on the 140-acre grounds.

All of Fred Seely's work paid off handsomely for him and Edwin W. Grove. In a matter of just a few years, the Grove Park Inn became one of the most popular vacation resorts in the country for wealthy Americans. The majority of the early guests came not for a few days of rest, but for several weeks or even months. Many arrived by train, bringing with them their favorite riding horses as well as their personal staff. Many others, such as Henry Ford and Thomas Edison, traveled in caravans of touring cars. Reservations were required months in advance; new guests had to be approved by Fred Seely before their reservations were accepted.

The publicity generated by the regular arrival of notable guests, such as Presidents Woodrow Wilson, Calvin Coolidge, and Herbert Hoover, entertainers Enrico Caruso, Harry Houdini, and Al Jolson, and industrialists Henry Ford, Thomas Edison, and Harvey Firestone, helped spread the fame of the Grove Park Inn.

Many of the famous guests at the inn Fred Seely had met either on one of his many trips or while serving as publisher of the Atlanta *Georgian*. He and Evelyn first met the Herbert Hoovers in China in 1901, when all four barely escaped during the Boxer Rebellion. Seely met Henry Ford when they were both struggling to make their mark in Detroit in the 1890s; he was introduced to Woodrow Wilson, then governor of New Jersey, at Princeton in 1912 and helped plan his successful Presidential campaign.

Whether it was an established friend or a new acquaintance, Fred Seely took it upon himself to personally entertain each of his famous guests, conducting a scenic auto tour of the area and a visit to Overlook Castle. According to an article that appeared in the Asheville *Citizen-Times* several years later, "Many a national figure was notified, on attempting to pay a bill at the Grove Park Inn, that he owed not a cent because the management was glad to have had him as its guest."

AMERICAN EXPEDITIONARY FORCES
OFFICE OF THE COMMANDER IN CHIEF

En route from
Asheville, N.C.,
February 20, 1920.

My dear Mr. Seely:

It was a great pleasure meeting you and Mrs. Seely during my brief visit to Asheville, and I desire to express my most cordial thanks to you both for the hospitality and courtesies which you accorded me and my Staff. I thoroughly enjoyed my short stay in your city, and especially the luncheon which you gave at the Grove Park Inn.

With warm regards and best wishes both for yourself and Mrs. Seely, believe me,

Sincerely yours,

John J. Pershing

Mr. Fred L. Seely,
Grove Park Inn,
Asheville, N.C.

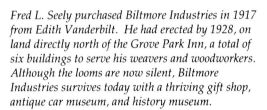

Fred L. Seely purchased Biltmore Industries in 1917 from Edith Vanderbilt. He had erected by 1928, on land directly north of the Grove Park Inn, a total of six buildings to serve his weavers and woodworkers. Although the looms are now silent, Biltmore Industries survives today with a thriving gift shop, antique car museum, and history museum.

Edwin W. Grove and his second wife, Gertrude, maintained a home in St. Petersburg, Florida, where this photograph was taken around 1918.

In April of 1917, Fred Seely purchased from Mrs. George Vanderbilt a small, but successful, Arts & Crafts enterprise called Biltmore Industries. Begun in 1901 under the patronage of Edith Vanderbilt, Biltmore Industries had evolved from a club for teenage woodcarvers into a cottage industry of weavers and woodworkers. By 1917 Biltmore Industries had outgrown its home in Biltmore Village. When Fred Seely revealed to Mrs. Vanderbilt his proposal to erect a number of new workshops for the craftsmen on thirty acres of land adjacent to the Grove Park Inn, she accepted his offer. The first building was completed that same year and by 1920 a total of forty-five looms were in constant operation. The weavers produced hundreds of yards of the finest homespun fabric in the world, eventually making Biltmore Industries as famous as its next door neighbor and proving that Fred Seely could organize, manage, and promote any enterprise he took an interest in.

During the early years of the Grove Park Inn, Edwin W. Grove continued to enlarge the web of his financial empire, buying property in Mexico, Texas, Arkansas, Tennessee, Missouri, West Virginia, Florida, the Carolinas, and Georgia, as well as owning a cattle company, a lumber mill, a coal company, several stone quarries, a motor car company, and a real estate company. Under his direction, the Paris Medicine Company continued to expand its tablet manufacturing division in St. Louis and opened a branch office in London. As predicted, sales of his large residential lots on and around Sunset Mountain accelerated after the opening of the Grove Park Inn, motivating Grove to make additional investments in Asheville real estate.

Grove continued to spend several months each year in Asheville, where local residents often saw him taking his customary walks. On an outing near the village of Swannanoa, twelve miles east of Asheville, he discovered an unusual deposit of stone, opening the door to yet another business, the Grove Gravel and Sand Company and, in the early twenties, Grovemont, E. W. Grove's model community. Another, more famous, instance occurred in 1922; it was related by Thomas Wolfe's brother, Frank, and recorded by Alexander Turnbull in his biography of the famous Asheville author:

One day, when Wolfe was home for the summer from Harvard, he and a friend borrowed a car to take two girls to the top of Sunset Mountain, and driving through Grove Estate a tire went flat.

They had begun their unaccustomed struggle with the spare when an elderly man in tan dungarees emerged from the forest and offered his services. With his aid the job was quickly done, and Tom handed him a quarter which he accepted with a bow....

Some years later, Tom's brother heard the story from the man himself; he was Grove, owner of the Grove Park Inn and the six thousand acres of Sunset Mountain. Frank asked if he had thought of returning the quarter. "No, I still have it," said Grove. "First, I kept it because it was the only tip I ever received, and then its preciousness grew in proportion to Tom's fame."

The success of the Grove Park Inn lured Edwin Grove into additional resort and hotel investments in Asheville. In 1920 Grove purchased The Albemarle Park Company, which included an English-style inn called The Manor and twenty large cottages grouped near the Grove Park Inn. Like the Grove Park Inn, The Manor depended on a wealthy clientele who stayed in Asheville for several weeks or months. Then, in 1922, Grove shocked the residents of the city by announcing plans to demolish the historic Battery Park Hotel, leveling the mountain across which it had sprawled since 1886, and erecting in its place a fourteen-story brick hotel. Both purchases were opposed by Fred Seely, who claimed they violated terms in his agreement with Grove. While the multi-millionaire publicly claimed that neither The Manor nor the new Battery Park Hotel would compete with the Grove Park Inn, no one was convinced. Family members recall that Edwin Grove had become increasingly jealous of his son-in-law's success at the Grove Park Inn, and speculate that the seventy-two-year-old Grove may have wanted to remind Seely and the people of Asheville of the power and money he controlled.

The twenty-year relationship of Edwin Grove and Fred Seely showed signs of deteriorating in 1921, when Grove dictated a new will. The 4500-word document provided explicit instructions for the disposition of his entire estate and personal belongings, down to his favorite watch and a monthly five-hundred-dollar payment to an illegitimate daughter. Conspicuous in its absence was any mention of the man who had once been like a son to Edwin Grove — Fred Seely. In addition to making no mention of Fred Seely in his will, Grove even went so far as to state in the document that the money and property which his daughter, Evelyn Grove Seely, would receive after his death "shall be for her sole control and management and free from any rights, interest or claims whatever on the part of any hus-

band or husbands, that she may at any time have." As evidence of the depth of the split with Seely, Grove further specified that upon Evelyn Grove Seely's death, her portion of the income generated by his trust was to pass directly to her children, not to her husband; in the event that none of her children were living at the time of her death, the will stipulated that the income which she had been receiving from the trust was to be granted to Edwin W. Grove, Jr., who was named executor of the trust and who was to retain the title of president of the Paris Medicine Company.

It is not clear when Fred Seely became aware of Grove's new will and the stipulation that virtually all of Grove's property, including the Paris Medicine Company and the Grove Park Inn, was to be placed upon his death into a trust to be managed by Edwin W. Grove, Jr. Although the income generated by the Grove trust was to be divided equally among Gertrude Grove, Edwin W. Grove, Jr., and Evelyn Grove Seely, Fred Seely felt betrayed. According to his descendants, Fred Seely had given Edwin W. Grove the patent rights to the tablet manufacturing machine which he had invented several years earlier. In exchange, according to Seely's claim, Grove had agreed "to transfer at his death a control in the medicine company to Mr. Seely, or if Mr. Seely should so elect, to transfer to him all other property owned by Mr. Grove, outside his holdings in the medicine company." Mr. Grove, it was set forth, agreed to do this because of "long and difficult services rendered in his behalf by Mr. Seely."

Three generations of Groves: Edwin W. Grove (1850-1927), Edwin W. Grove, Jr. (1890-1934), and Edwin W. Grove, III (1912-1967).

(Previous page) Installed in 1919, this Skinner organ provided guests with music until 1927, when Fred Seely, its owner, left the inn. The mahogany case had been carved by his workers at Biltmore Industries. The animal heads were a gift from William Jennings Bryan, who bought them while out West.

(Below) Rustic gates marked the entrance to the inn until the 1970s, when they were deemed unnecessary. The first line of the sign reads "Sightseers either on foot or in automobiles are requested not to go beyond these gates."

In December of 1925, Fred Seely filed a lawsuit in St. Louis against his father-in-law, attempting to force Grove to honor Seely's claim of an earlier agreement granting Seely, upon Grove's death, ownership of the Grove Park Inn as well as other Grove property. The suit, which involved an estimated five to six million dollars in real estate, was still pending when, on January 27, 1927, the seventy-six year-old Edwin Wiley Grove died of pneumonia in his suite at the Battery Park Hotel. When the multimillionaire's will was officially filed the following week, it became painfully clear that Edwin Grove did not want Fred Seely to be associated with the Grove Park Inn after his death. In addition to assigning William V. Curran,

Grove's private secretary and formerly the secretary-treasurer of the Paris Medicine Company, the responsibility of "full control and management of all my real estate and other properties in the States of North Carolina, Georgia, and Florida," Grove also declared that his investments in North Carolina, including the Grove Park Inn, are a "permanent investment and [I] desire that they not be put on the market and sold as a whole or in part." Shortly afterwards, Edwin W. Grove, Jr., and William V. Curran informed Fred Seely that upon the expiration of his lease on December 31, 1927, his services would no longer be needed at the Grove Park Inn.

Through his marriage to Edwin Grove's daughter, Fred Seely was destined to receive a portion of the estimated ten million dollar estate he had helped to build, but Grove had instructed his executors to place the majority of his investments in a trust and to dispense the income in equal amounts on a monthly or quarterly basis to three individuals: his wife, Gertrude, his son, Edwin, and his daughter by his first marriage, Evelyn. According to the will, upon the death of his wife, Gertrude, the net annual income from all of the properties, investments, and businesses held in the Grove trust was to be divided equally between Edwin and Evelyn. Only a few months after her husband's death, Gertrude Grove requested in cash and property the equivalent of one third of the ten million dollar estate. Her request was submitted to the executor, Edwin W. Grove, Jr., and approved. In 1928, at the age of sixty-seven, Gertrude Mathewson Grove died, but not before having willed the bulk of her personal estate, including an estimated three million dollars recently drawn from her late husband's trust, to her only natural child, Edwin W. Grove, Jr. In a letter written nearly twenty years later, Evelyn Grove Seely remarked, "As you remember, Mama Grove broke my father's will, but that was perfectly all right as I received far more than I deserved and I am certain that it was never intended for my children to have great wealth. It is far better for them to work and earn [and] possess sympathy with those who must balance the budget."

As his lease on the Grove Park Inn drew to a close, the fifty-six-year-old Fred Seely prepared for yet another major change in his life. Anticipating such a day, perhaps, Seely had made the decision years earlier to keep Biltmore Industries beyond the grasp of Edwin W. Grove. In 1927, after notification that his lease would not be renewed, Seely constructed three additional buildings for his craftsmen. That December he moved his office from the great inn — to which he had dedicated sixteen years of his life — to Biltmore Industries, which would become his primary business interest throughout the remainder of his life. One of his final duties was the disposition of the famous Skinner organ, which had entertained thousands of his guests in the Great Hall. Though he had once considered moving the gigantic organ to Overlook Castle, he finally accepted an offer for the organ from the First Presbyterian Church in Baltimore, Maryland. The Skinner organ remained in that church until 1961, when it was dismantled and sold to an unidentified party.

The first and most glamorous era of the Grove Park Inn came to an end with the death of Edwin W. Grove and the departure of Fred Seely. Although Edwin Grove had provided the land, the money, and the materials for the hotel that bore his name, it remained for Fred Seely to provide the philosophy, the leadership, and the vision which guided the Grove Park Inn to greatness. Neither man could have known that within months of their departure, events that would shake the financial footing of the entire world would threaten the very existence of the inn which they both, in their own fashion, had worked so hard to build.

It will be the policy of the new owners to promote a better friendship between the inn and the people of this city and to give it a more important and active place in the life of the community.

Isaac "Ike" Hall
October 28, 1943

DECLINE AND DECAY:
1928 - 1955

The departure of Fred L. Seely from the Grove Park Inn on January 1, 1928, came at the worst possible time for the world-famous hotel. Rumors of an impending economic earthquake were already being whispered privately, despite public reassurances from President Calvin Coolidge to the contrary. From their offices in St. Louis, Edwin W. Grove, Jr., and William V. Curran, trustees of the ten million dollar Grove estate, appointed Martin H. Burke as the new general manager of the Grove Park Inn. It quickly became apparent that the trustees had no intention of honoring Edwin W. Grove's final request that his real estate empire in Asheville, including twelve hundred acres of land, the Grove Arcade, the Battery Park Hotel, the Albemarle Park Company, and the Grove Park Inn, "be not put on the market and sold as whole or in part."

On September 22, 1927, less than eight months after Grove's death, Edwin W. Grove, Jr., and William Curran announced their decision to sell the Grove Park Inn. By the spring of 1928, John S. Adams, an Asheville attorney who had been named commissioner of the sale, had found a buyer. On the first day of May, Gertrude Grove endorsed the sale, justified, as the trustees claimed, since "it became necessary to sell portions of the real estate belonging to the said E. W. Grove ... for the purpose of making assets to pay debts." When no challengers came forward, the court approved the trustees' request to sell the inn. While no listing of debts of the estate was required, the pharmaceutical and real estate empires which Edwin W. Grove had worked fifty-three years to build clearly stood on solid ground. Though Fred Seely's lawsuit against the Grove estate was still pending, the only apparent major debt the trustees had to settle was the unprecedented request by Gertrude Grove — who was to die a few months later — for one-third of the estimated ten million dollar trust in cash.

On September 10, 1936, President Franklin D. Roosevelt (with hat in hand) left the inn to address a crowd of over twenty thousand people at McCormick Field. To the right of F.D.R. is Asheville Mayor Robert M. Wells and Governor J.C.B. Ehringhaus. John Roosevelt, the president's son, is seated across from the three men.

In a series of complicated legal maneuvers, the trustees agreed in March of 1928 to sell the Grove Park Inn to T. E. Hambleton and Donald McKnew, owners of a Baltimore-based brokerage firm, for approximately one million dollars. On May 1, after receiving a quitclaim deed from Gertrude Grove, the property was transferred from Hambleton and McKnew to the newly formed Grove Park Inn, Inc., "a corporation organized and existing under laws of Maryland and comprising Baltimore banking interests." The new owners shouldered a sizable debt: they borrowed $300,000 from the Continental Trust Company of Baltimore, to which they added $225,000 from undisclosed sources to pay the Grove estate $525,000. The balance of $475,000 took the form of a first mortgage with the St. Louis Union Trust Company, a co-trustee of the Grove estate.

Guests arriving at the inn shortly after it opened made their way down the same rock-lined road that guests still use today.

The new owners made numerous changes in the Grove Park Inn over the course of the next few years. Recognizing a need to enlarge their clientele to include traveling businessmen and corporate conventions, many of the changes ran counter to the austere philosophy by which Fred Seely had governed the inn and its guests for fourteen years. The Writing Room in the south wing was remodeled into the Card Room; two of the original four Ladies' Parlors adjacent to it became meeting rooms. A beauty parlor was added next to the barber shop in the lower level. The three-lane bowling alley on the west side of the lower level was removed and the room renamed the Convention Hall, "available for meetings, dances or special parties," though the billiard tables remained for the time being. One of the most radical changes involved the original forty-foot indoor swimming pool, which was removed. The pool area was remodeled to become the Bath Department, with "expert technicians in charge [and] separate rooms for men and women." A 1935 brochure explained that "the Grove Park Inn Baths have been added to the equipment of Grove Park Inn in order that our guests may have the advantage of health-building facilities without the inconvenience and expense of hospital treatment." Reflecting a growing interest in the game of golf, the management installed an outdoor miniature golf course opposite the east entrance. The staff also invented a game called "Obstacle Golf," designed to be played inside the Great Hall. And, in yet another move intended to attract families and their children to the inn, the owners elected to make two of the inn's most elite cottages, the Ann Hathaway (later re-named the Presidential Cottage) and the Van Dyke cottages, available "for families and special parties."

Though they believed Fred Seely's methods of managing the hotel outdated, the new owners did not harbor toward him the same animosity Edwin W. Grove, Jr., and William Curran had clearly demonstrated. Seely's Biltmore Industries maintained a news and cigar stand in the Great Hall where his staff also sold "the famous Biltmore Homespun, wood carving, bronze and silver novelties," including Roycroft products. A second shop in the Great Hall, featured "hooked rugs, counterpanes, linens, linsey-woolsey, pottery, pewter, handmade furniture, hand wrought iron, mica lamp shades and other handmade products of this mountain region."

By the early forties, the wicker furniture had been replaced by oak "paddle-arm" couches and chairs. The Roycroft chandeliers had been altered by this date, but the stone columns remained intact. Note the gift shop to the far right.

Despite Seely's absence, the Grove Park Inn continued to provide accommodations for famous guests. President Herbert Hoover stayed briefly in 1930 and 1931, when he journeyed to Asheville to visit his son, recuperating from tuberculosis at the Blue Briar Cottage on Sunset Mountain. Former President William Howard Taft, who was then Chief Justice of the Supreme Court, made plans to arrive at the Grove Park Inn on January 15, 1930, where "he hoped the balmy air which he expects to find in Asheville will in a few weeks restore his strength." According to the Seely family and the Asheville *Citizen*, Fred Seely, as well as several other prominent residents, had offered Chief Justice Taft the use of his home and staff for as long as he wished, but the former President declined, stating that it might seem inappropriate for the Chief Justice of the Supreme Court "to accept any favor which might obligate him to anyone." Even if Taft had been unaware of it, his staff undoubtedly knew that Fred Seely's well-publicized lawsuit over his father-in-law's will was pending in a St. Louis circuit court.

As the twenty-seventh President (1909-1913), Taft had tipped the scales at a much publicized three hundred and twenty pounds. When the seventy-three-year-old Republican arrived at the Grove Park Inn in 1930, he still weighed a robust two hundred and forty pounds, but his failing health restricted him to little more than a daily walk and a short ride in his custom-designed automobile. Despite the soothing Asheville climate and the efforts of Dr. Paul Ringer, his local physician, Chief Justice Taft's condition worsened. Sensing that death was imminent, he returned to Washington, D.C. in February, where he died of heart disease on March 8, 1930.

Despite the publicity generated by famous politicians, entertainers, and artists, the Grove Park Inn could not escape the repercussions of the stock market crash of 1929. The Great Depression paralyzed the nation, including the two groups of people on whom the Grove Park Inn had come to depend: the established wealthy class and a growing business class. Without the leadership of a general manager of Fred Seely's caliber, the Grove Park Inn faltered. On January 15, 1932, the Grove Park Inn, Inc., defaulted on both its first mortgage to the St. Louis Union Trust Company and its second mortgage to the Continental Trust Company. Buncombe County Judge Hoyle Sink appointed the First National Bank and Trust Company of Asheville as receiver for the resort, while the stockholders attempted to reorganize and refinance their two existing mortgages totalling $711,500. R. H. McDuffie, vice president of the First National Bank and Trust Company, supervised the Grove Park Inn during this period and appointed Albert N. Barnett as acting general manager. In October of 1932, a holding company comprising second mortgage bondholders and Baltimore banking interests

The original stable was located northeast of the present Sports Center. It was remodeled into an automobile garage in 1924 and later demolished. (S.H. Research Center)

Fresh, meticulously prepared foods have always been a priority at the Grove Park Inn. Shown here is the original kitchen before the addition of the two new dining facilities.

purchased the title to the Grove Park Inn from the St. Louis Union Trust Company and the Continental Trust Company. George G. Shriver, one of the principal stockholders in the 1928 purchase, became president of the new corporation. Shriver announced that acting manager Albert Barnett was to become general manager of the inn, due to the fact that "since the bank took over the property last January, an operating profit of more than $40,000 has been realized."

Under Barnett's leadership, the Grove Park Inn maintained a steady course for the remainder of the decade. Had the stockholders of the Grove Park Inn corporation not been saddled with a high pre-Depression mortgage, the Grove Park Inn might well have operated smoothly despite the hardships of the thirties. As it was, Albert Barnett came close to restoring the luster that Fred L. Seely had originally provided. The two men became close friends and, in many ways, Barnett attempted to emulate the ideals and philosophy of Fred Seely.

As both the country and the Grove Park Inn slowly healed, wealthy guests began returning to Asheville. Among the most famous were President Franklin D. Roosevelt and first lady Eleanor Roosevelt, though, true to form, their visits to North Carolina did not coincide. Eleanor Roosevelt traveled by car through the Asheville region in July of 1934, "in her quest for information on the hand-weaving crafts." She and her female traveling companions stayed at the Grove Park Inn, where they were greeted by Fred Seely, who served as their host. After a morning swim in the Asheville Country Club pool, Mrs. Roosevelt was given a tour of Biltmore Industries. Fred Seely then provided the people of Asheville an opportunity to see the nation's first lady by taking a preannounced route through the city on their drive to Tryon, where they visited the famed Tryon Weavers, as well as the Tryon Toymakers.

Eleanor Roosevelt returned to Asheville and the Grove Park Inn in April of 1937, when, once again, she was on a motor tour of North Carolina, Tennessee, and South Carolina. Like Edith Vanderbilt some forty years earlier, Eleanor Roosevelt took a great interest in the craftsmen and women of the Blue Ridge and Great Smoky Mountains, and, as on her previous visit, Fred Seely served as her host and tour guide.

In 1933, President Franklin D. Roosevelt had signed a bill which provided 1.5 million dollars for the development of the recently established Great Smoky Mountains National Park. Three years later, Roosevelt toured the Great Smoky Mountains, arriving at the Grove Park Inn on the evening of September 10, 1936. General Manager Albert Barnett had set aside fifty rooms for the President and his staff, which included sixteen Secret Service agents. The following day Asheville schools, stores, and businesses closed, as an estimated fifty thousand people lined the streets from the Grove Park Inn to McCormick Field, where another twenty thousand people had waited since six o'clock that morning to listen to the President's mid-day address. From his open limousine parked at home plate, President Roosevelt delivered a brief but stirring tribute to the people and the region of Tennessee and North Carolina before continuing on his journey to Charlotte.

Ironically, one of the most tragic figures ever to stay at the Grove Park Inn may well have been watching from his fourth floor window as President Roosevelt's motorcade pulled away from the Grove Park Inn that morning. Novelist F. Scott Fitzgerald, once crowned the chronicler of the Jazz Age, found himself and his novels out of tune during the Depression years. In 1935, after doctors discovered a suspicious spot on his lung, Fitzgerald sought refuge in Asheville, where he hoped to revive his health and the literary brilliance that years earlier had produced *This Side of Paradise* (1920) and *The Great Gatsby* (1925). The thirty-nine-year-old author arrived in Asheville "sick, debt-ridden, and despairing"; only the generosity of his friends and publisher enabled him to live at the elegant Grove Park Inn in rooms 441 and 443 during the summer of 1935. Plagued with insurmountable debt and gnawing self-doubt, Fitzgerald could produce only a few mediocre short stories during his stay in Asheville.

Novelist F. Scott Fitzgerald and the Grove Park Inn both fell on hard times during the late thirties. Fitzgerald lived at the inn during the summers of 1935 and 1936. In 1936, his wife, Zelda, was a patient at nearby Highland Hospital.

Fitzgerald returned to the Grove Park Inn in 1936, when he transferred his wife Zelda, who for years had been hospitalized with advanced schizophrenia, to Highland Hospital. Despite having Zelda nearby, Fitzgerald slipped into his old habits; showing off on an outing at Beaver Lake, he severely dislocated his shoulder attempting a fifteen-foot dive and was confined for weeks in an uncomfortable cast. He tried unsuccessfully to dictate stories to a secretary, but, as she recounted, "His usual pattern was to start out having pots of black coffee served to us at intervals, but as the morning progressed into afternoon and the pain and the stress increased, he would advance to stronger stuff. At the end of the session he would slump over, overcome by exhaustion and drink."

By the end of the summer Fitzgerald was growing desperate. A young woman with whom he had been having an affair at the Grove Park Inn had returned to her husband. His manuscripts and his pleas for advances were being met with rejections. Zelda's condition was deteriorating, and their visits together were becoming tense and infrequent. On September 24, 1936, his fortieth birthday, Fitzgerald consented to an interview with a New York *Post* reporter; anticipating a favorable review of his long-awaited comeback, Fitzgerald was devastated to read his literary obituary. A few hours later he attempted suicide by swallowing a phial of morphine, but was revived by his nurse and a local physician. Fitzgerald remained at the inn until that winter, when he moved in with friends in Tryon. In the spring of 1937, he journeyed to Hollywood, where he tried unsuccessfully to become a screenwriter. Though he appeared to be taking control of his life, the damage done by years of alcohol abuse could not be overcome. On December 21, 1940, forty-four-year-old F. Scott Fitzgerald suffered a fatal heart attack. As an ending to his tragic story, eight years later a fire destroyed Highland Hospital, killing seven patients trapped on the top floor. Zelda Fitzgerald, who was to be released the next week, was included among the dead.

While visits to the Grove Park Inn by public figures such as Franklin and Eleanor Roosevelt, Wiley Post and Will Rogers, and Bill Tilden and Bobby Jones, generated invaluable publicity for the Grove Park Inn, an increasing number of private individuals began taking short vacations at the resort. Typical of this growing clientele was a young couple from Kentucky, who stayed for two nights in October of 1936 on their honeymoon journey to Florida. Forty-five years later the woman wrote back: "What do I remember about the Grove Park Inn? The beautiful setting and grounds, our luxurious room, the elegant dining room, fine luscious silver, and service. In the elevator there was always a big basket of delicious apples! A silly thing to remember. I guess, however, it just seems one of all the many, even small, details the inn provided for our comfort. It was indeed a 'Grand' hotel."

As war clouds hovered on the horizon, the Grove Park Inn struggled to remain profitable. In 1938, the directors of the corporation were forced to restructure their mortgage debt with the St. Louis Union Trust Company; two years later, the Grove Park Inn corporation borrowed $100,000 from the Jefferson Standard Life Insurance Company of Greensboro, North Carolina, and instituted an ambitious, though cosmetic, remodeling program. The Francis Marion room, earlier a part of the dining room and presently the Vanderbilt Wing connector, was remodeled to serve as the inn's cocktail lounge.

Oak "paddle-arm" chairs and couches were purchased from a lodge in Illinois to replace the aging wicker furniture in the lobby. The owners also felt the Great Hall needed more light, but rather than supplementing the original twelve solid-copper Roycroft chandeliers, workmen removed and discarded their rounded, copper pans and replaced them with flat, frosted-glass panels. As the crowning touch to their disfigurement, four medieval fleurs-de-lis were attached to each chandelier in an attempt to duplicate the interior of a European castle.

The inn's first cocktail lounge was located by 1935 in what is now the Vanderbilt Wing connector. Formerly called the Francis Marion room, it remained a cocktail lounge until the arrival of the Jack Tar Hotels management.

Additional plans for the inn were set aside in December of 1941, when the United States Congress declared war on the Axis powers of Germany, Italy, Hungary, and Japan. The United States government quickly moved to house, under armed guard, Axis diplomats and their families who had been living in the United States. Several hundred diplomats were interned at The Homestead Hotel in Hot Springs, Virginia, and The Greenbrier Hotel in White Sulphur Springs, West Virginia. When it became apparent that additional housing would be required, agents from the Federal Bureau of Investigation inspected the Grove Park Inn, declaring it and its staff suitable for their needs. The terms of the agreement between the government and the hotel were simple: in return for providing rooms and meals for the diplomats and their families, the owners of the inn would be guaranteed eight dollars a day for adults and five dollars a day for children for a minimum of 225 persons. According to a story in the Asheville *Times*, the diplomats would be paying for their accommodations from foreign bank accounts frozen and controlled by the United States government. The management of the Grove Park Inn would not be allowed to accept outside guests during the time in which the government leased the hotel.

On April 3, 1942, with no prior public announcement, two trains arrived in Asheville with 242 Italian, Hungarian, and Bulgarian diplomats, their families, and, in many cases, their private staffs. As a reporter noted, it seemed evident from their clothing, luggage, and servants that the new guests at the Grove Park Inn were accustomed to luxurious surroundings. Approximately forty-eight local men were hired to guard the nineteen-acre grounds. The area they patrolled was not delineated by barbed wire, but extra lights had been installed and the guards were armed. The diplomats and their families were permitted to roam the grounds freely, making use of the same facilities, with the exception of the Asheville Country Club golf course, that hotel guests used during normal times.

As expected, the United States government had begun negotiating the exchange of diplomats with the Axis powers even before the diplomats and their families arrived at the Grove Park Inn. The majority of the diplomats were quietly transported out of Asheville on May 5, 1942, but less than two weeks later they were replaced by 63 Japanese and 155 Germans and their families, none of whom were ranking diplomats. Security was tightened for this second group of internees at the Grove Park Inn, either as a reflection of their perceived threat or of the scars already left by the terrible war. By the middle of June, all but 23 of the Axis diplomats and nationals had been transferred from the Grove Park Inn in preparation for their journey home; those that remained had requested to remain in the United States and were soon transported to appropriate locations.

Before it was demolished, this small gas station was located at the intersection northeast of the present Sports Center, where it serviced hotel vehicles. This photograph was taken around 1939.

From his office at Biltmore Industries, Fred Seely had watched with great concern as the new owners, the Depression, and the war took their toll on the Grove Park Inn. On the morning of March 14, 1942, at the age of seventy, Fred Seely died. Several hundred citizens paid their last respects at Overlook Castle to a man the *Citizen-Times* called "A City-Builder."

The people of Asheville mourned the loss of one of Asheville's leading businessmen and wealthiest residents with no less sympathy and appreciation than they had demonstrated upon the death of his father-in-law fifteen years earlier. Seely's last years had been spent renovating the Battery Park Hotel, which he and his wife had been deeded in 1940 by the St. Louis

Wartime romances blossomed on the terrace with the arrival of naval officers in Asheville during 1942 and 1943.

Union Trust Company to settle the lawsuit Seely had filed against Edwin W. Grove in 1925. In his obituary, Seely was praised for having convinced the owners of the American Enka Corporation to establish their plant in Asheville, for having donated to local charities "the equivalent of several sizable fortunes," and for having dedicated thirty years of his life to the welfare of the city in which he had lived since his arrival in 1912.

In the summer of 1942, the staff at the Grove Park Inn worked to prepare the resort for their summer trade, but even before the departure of the last of the Axis diplomats came the confirmation that the United States Navy intended to lease the hotel beginning in October. That fall the inn became a rest and rehabilitation center for naval aviation officers under the direction of Lieutenant-Commander J. B. Sutherland. The staff at the Grove Park Inn and general manager Burton S. Frei greeted the first group of officers, whose stays would range from a few days to several weeks. The Navy first intended to use the inn as a "rest and recreation center... to prevent casualties, particularly nervous casualties," but it became necessary to temporarily house wounded seamen while the Appalachian Hall on the old Kenilworth Inn property was being transformed into a military convalescent center. Once again, the grounds of the Grove Park Inn were patrolled by guards, but this time their primary duty was to prevent curious citizens from disturbing the naval officers and injured sailors.

The United States Navy relinquished control of the Grove Park Inn on June 1, 1943. Shortly thereafter, the St. Louis Union Trust Company, which, as the original first mortgage holder, had been forced to foreclose on the property shortly before the war, sought a buyer for the 142-room hotel. On October 27, 1943, it was announced that Isaac "Ike" Hall, an Oklahoma City businessman, who had made his fortune in oil and real estate developments, had purchased the inn. While the purchase price was not officially disclosed, Hall reportedly paid $230,000 for the thirty-year-old hotel.

The following spring, Ike Hall and the Grove Park Inn basked in the glow of publicity surrounding the announcement that Manuel L. Quezon, the Philippine president-in-exile, had selected the resort for a month-long period of rest and relaxation. He and his family had barely escaped Japanese invaders in 1942 and, at the invitation of President Roosevelt, had established the headquarters of the Philippine government in Washington, D.C. President Quezon, his family, and his private staff had spent the winter of 1943 in Miami, but arrived at the Grove Park Inn on April 19, 1944, where they established temporary headquarters for the Philippine government in the Ann Hathaway cottage (now known as the Presidential Cottage). Quezon, who suffered from a lung ailment, was transported from the railway station to the Grove Park Inn by ambulance. He and a small staff officially operated their government-in-exile from the Grove Park Inn until mid-June, when they returned to Washington to await the end of the war.

Asheville citizens awoke Sunday morning, July 23, 1944, to a double-banner headline in the *Citizen-Times* announcing the federal government's decision to turn Asheville's four largest hotels into a redistribution center for returning combat soldiers. As the paper reported, "Asheville was chosen as the site for the center to serve the Southeast because of its splendid year-around climate and because it is one of the outstanding and most beautiful resort cities in Eastern America. The center will be one of more than a score throughout the nation." The four hotels were the George Vanderbilt, the Asheville-Biltmore, the Battery Park, and the Grove Park Inn. The redistribution center was to provide a relaxing atmosphere for soldiers of the Army ground forces, including infantry, artillery, and armored units, who had spent a minimum of forty-five days in combat duty. Most of these men and women had not seen their families since first entering the military service. All personnel, the army emphasized, would be "physically and mentally well."

Qualifying soldiers first received a twenty-one-day furlough to visit their homes, then were ordered to report to one of the redistribution centers for ten to fourteen days for physical examinations, paperwork, back pay, and reassignment to noncombat duty. They were allowed to bring their husbands or wives with them to Asheville, where they could use the complete facilities of the Asheville Country Club. Most of the officers assigned to Asheville beginning in September of 1944 were housed at the Grove Park Inn, as were the majority of the soldiers who were accompanied by their husbands or wives. In writing about the inn, the *Citizen-Times* observed that "in recent years it has been operated much more on the general hotel pattern, with conventions not infrequently held there, but the Grove Park Inn still caters to the better class. The inn, in addition to providing the finest of accommodations, will continue to operate the riding stables, skeet range, miniature golf, tennis courts and other recreational facilities on its grounds and will also handle the contracts of the Asheville Country Club course privileges for the soldiers and their wives desiring to play golf."

Sunset Hall (1913-1990) stood northwest of the present Sports Center, where for several decades it housed many Grove Park Inn employees from the housekeeping, kitchen and maintenance staffs. (S. H. Research Center)

Though Asheville was justifiably proud of its patriotic spirit, not everyone was pleased with the manner in which "the representatives of the War Department came and saw and took." In a *Citizen-Times* editorial that followed the announcement, the newspaper pointed out that the influx of hundreds of military personnel would "strain to the breaking point our already overtaxed housing, eating and transportation facilities," as well as close the doors of the city to the tourist trade on which it had grown to depend. Hundreds of guests in the city's four largest hotels were asked to vacate their rooms, and hundreds more were notified that their reservations had been cancelled. While the staffs at the hotels, including the Grove Park Inn, which was being managed by Burton Frei, remained intact, many of the businesses and shops located within them were forced to close.

For Ike Hall, the Oklahoma businessman who now owned the Grove Park Inn, the arrival of the military in 1944 was a stroke of financial good fortune. With no experience and little interest in hotel management, Hall had neither the background nor the incentive to compete with the growing number of Asheville hotels catering to tourists, conventions, wealthy vacationers, and public officials. The contract with the United States government, which kept the Grove Park Inn filled with officers, enlisted men, and their wives through the end of the war in September of 1945, stipulated that the government had to refurbish the hotel in preparation for its return to civilian use. In 1946, Hall leased the inn to the Abraham Sonnabend interests, which, while operating the hotel under general manager H.L. Thomas, made no major changes or improvements in the structure. The owners did attempt to maintain the former image of the inn, advertising in 1949 that they "have an excellent orchestra which plays during luncheons, dinner and for dancing each evening." For the first time since 1912, however, the Grove Park Inn was closed during the winter months, opening from April until early November from 1946 through 1951.

The military did return one final time, though in a far less disruptive manner, when on April 13, 1947, General Dwight D. Eisenhower, then chief of staff of the United States Army, and his wife, Mamie, arrived at the Grove Park Inn for an overnight stay. General Eisenhower had just completed a fourteen-day inspection tour of Army installations in several Southern states and remained in virtual seclusion during his brief visit at the hotel. It was not until after the military entourage had departed that general manager H. L. Thomas confirmed that the general and his wife had stayed at the inn's Ann Hathaway cottage.

In the years following the war and the departure of the Sonnabend group in 1950, the Grove Park Inn depended solely on its reputation as a fine hostelry, for, as its fortieth birthday approached, owner Ike Hall neither promoted nor improved the aging structure. Hall, described by many as a big, rough cowboy, ran the inn from his office in the Great Hall or from the Ann Hathaway cottage, where he and his family lived. Unable to get along with any of his managers, Hall ran the inn himself, opening it year-round beginning in 1952, but he never seemed happy there. He began attempting to sell it as soon the Sonnabend corporation departed, but his asking price and the deteriorating condition of the inn frightened off any potential investors. Despite his personal unhappiness, Ike Hall sponsored "Dollar Dances" at the Grove Park Inn every Saturday night, charging only one dollar for anyone who wanted to enjoy the music and dance.

As the country and Asheville adjusted to both a new decade and a changing post-war era, the Grove Park Inn struggled to survive. Much of what had made her great — modern facilities, solid management, and a reputation for fine service — had eroded since the departure of Fred L. Seely twenty-two years earlier. Though her granite walls appeared impervious to age, little had been done to update or maintain the water, plumbing, and electrical lines within them. The oak furniture, French rugs, and imported linens, which fifty years earlier had been the best that money could buy, now were worn, soiled and stained. Neither old enough to be considered quaint nor new enough to be called modern, the Grove Park Inn was no longer the pride of Asheville. A growing number of conventions, tourists, entertainers, and politicians were opting not to stay there. Local merchants watched nervously as the inn's unpaid bills accumulated, until most began demanding cash before a delivery would be made. By 1954, it seemed that Ike Hall might never find a buyer, and the fate of the Grove Park Inn remained uncertain. Those who had closely inspected the inn and accurately assessed her deteriorating condition were not optimistic. The Grove Park Inn, many predicted, would soon close its doors.

The arrival of General Eisenhower on April 13, 1947, was kept secret until after he and his wife had left the inn the following day.

I was entranced with the idea of the thing, the uniqueness of the big, uncut stones, and one unusual touch – a big bowl of apples in the lobby for the guests. But I bought it primarily because we liked Asheville so much.

Charles A. Sammons
April 29, 1984

THE LONG CLIMB:
1955 - 1978

The opening of the cloverleaf-shaped pool in 1956 and the Fairway Motor Lodge (to right, out of picture) in 1958 signaled the beginning of a new era for the Grove Park Inn.

On August 10, 1955, Ed Leach, president of the Jack Tar Hotels corporation in Dallas, Texas, flew into Asheville to bid on the Battery Park Hotel, which was being sold by the sons of Fred L. Seely. That noon, Leach left the courthouse where the sale was being conducted, rented a car, and drove out to see the Grove Park Inn, which he had heard about many years earlier, but never seen.

As he turned off Macon Avenue and drove down the stone-lined drive leading to the entrance, Leach couldn't help but notice a rather bedraggled man, dressed in an old pair of dungarees and an undershirt, sitting with a bottle of bourbon in his hand on the front steps of the Ann Hathaway cottage. Leach parked his car in the deserted lot and walked into the cavernous Great Hall, which, except for a very dignified bellman, was nearly empty. "The place was gloomy," he later recalled. "The drapes were dusty, the furniture old. It didn't look like a thing had been done to it since 1913. I walked around, had a meager lunch in the dining room, and, like any good hotel man, started asking questions. When the old bellman let it be known that the place was for sale, I asked 'Where's the owner?'"

"Up there," he replied, pointing out the door, "sittin' out front of his cottage."

It didn't take Ed Leach long to figure out that Ike Hall was an unhappy man. He had owned the Grove Park Inn since 1944, but for five years had been trying unsuccessfully to find a buyer for the old hotel. His wife had already moved back to Oklahoma with their two small girls, one of whom suffered from asthma, and Ike was anxious to join them. That afternoon Ike Hall drove Ed Leach around the hotel grounds and introduced him to Harry Blomberg, an Asheville businessman who had purchased and saved Biltmore Industries in 1953. "If the right kind of people got ahold of that old hotel," Blomberg told Leach, "it could make money." Later that afternoon, Leach phoned his boss, Charles Sammons, in Dallas. "Mr. Sammons," he said, "you got to come up here."

The fifty-seven-year-old Charles Sammons trusted Ed Leach's judgment, but he didn't rush down to Asheville to meet Ike Hall, for, in addition to being a shrewd businessman, Charles Sammons already knew about the Grove Park Inn.

Sammons had been born on June 5, 1898 in Ardmore, Oklahoma. Orphaned at the age of eleven, he and his two sisters were sent in 1909 to live with an aunt in Plano, Texas. After graduation from high school, the enterprising Sammons started his first business, selling carloads of hay and grain. He quickly established both a fine reputation and a line of credit with the Security National Bank, even though he was not yet of legal age. Sammons soon expanded both his knowledge and his business, taking courses in bookkeeping and business law, then branching out into cotton speculation. By 1928, at the age of thirty-one, Sammons had accumulated a sizable savings, but the depression wiped out Security National Bank and all of Sammons' money.

Undaunted, the young entrepreneur and his new bride, Rosine, moved to Waco, Texas, where he began rebuilding his finances in the cotton business. While in Waco he met two future partners who had experience in the field of insurance, but who, like Sammons, had been set back by the depression. The three formed the Postal Indemnity Company, an insurance business, which they soon moved to Dallas. While his two partners built the sales force, Sammons took charge of the organization of the young company. Years later, he remarked that, although he had made his fortune in the insurance business, he never sold a single policy. "I guess the closest thing I did to selling was to convince a few Dallas banks to lend me money when I needed it."

Under Sammons' direction, the Postal Indemnity Company quickly grew by expanding its territory and by acquiring other mutual insurance businesses, several in states other than Texas. By 1938, however, the partnership had dissolved; after the death of one of the men, Sammons' other partner decided to move to Indiana to run one of the insurance companies the three had acquired in that state. Sammons remained in Texas, where that year he founded the Reserve Life Insurance Company. Once Reserve Life was established, Sammons expanded again, building an accident and health insurance branch that grew quickly during the war era. Although a heart attack in 1948 threatened his life, Sammons rebounded with characteristic energy. As the nation settled into the fifties, Charles Sammons, not unlike Edwin Grove some forty years earlier, was ready to expand his financial empire into new fields.

When Sammons learned, in the early fifties, that the eighty-five-room Jack Tar Hotel in Galveston, Texas, was for sale, he decided to buy it, in part because he, his wife, and their daughter, had often stayed there. Sammons enjoyed the challenges presented by the hotel business, and within a few years had purchased or constructed hotels in Charleston, South Carolina; Marathon and Clearwater, Florida; and Orange, Texas. Ed Leach, the former manager of the original Jack Tar Hotel in Galveston, quickly became Sammons' associate and president of the rapidly growing Jack Tar Hotels corporation. As Leach explained, "Mr. Sammons loved to set up companies and then make someone president. He had nearly a dozen at one time, just like me, but he always made it a point to keep in touch with all of his projects."

Ed Leach arranged a Sunday morning meeting in Dallas between Ike Hall and Charles Sammons in September of 1955. Though anxious to sell the aging Grove Park Inn, Ike Hall was convinced that it was worth $650,000. Sammons, pointing out that the inn now had only 142 guest rooms, 35 without a private bath, offered Hall $400,000. By noon, when Hall had to leave for the airport, the asking price for the Grove Park Inn was down to $500,000, but Sammons remained adamant. When it became apparent the two men could not reach an agreement, Sammons offered to drive Ike Hall to the Dallas airport, where, in the men's room, he made one final pitch. "Ike," he said, "how about $450,000 — in cash?"

Ike thought for a moment, then said, "I'll take it."

The announcement of the sale, which was officially completed on September 28, 1955, was accompanied by a statement by Ed Leach that Jack Tar Hotels intended to immediately invest more than $100,000 in renovations in the forty-two-year-old hotel. Sammons and his wife visited the inn a few weeks later, as plans were being formulated for the project. The inn was closed that winter, as workmen, under the direction of Leach and newly appointed general manager George

Although it proved popular in 1958, the Fairway Lodge soon became outdated and was demolished in 1982 to make way for the more harmonious and much larger Sammons Wing.

Stobie, undertook the first major renovation of the Grove Park Inn. Looking back, Leach explained, "We made a lot of changes and a few mistakes, but it was 1955 and we wanted to bring people back to the Grove Park Inn. People didn't care about historic old hotels then. They wanted new, modern motels and we had to recognize that. We decided that the stone columns in the lobby were dust-catchers, so I got ahold of a Miami decorator — or, I should say, a Miami decorator got ahold of me — and talked me into covering the columns."

The granite pillars in the Great Hall became giant oval columns in 1955, as the interior decorators attempted to modernize the hotel.

At the center of each of the six columns in the Great Hall is a square, solid-concrete core supporting the weight of the roof. Before stonemasons applied the granite facing in 1913, the plumbers and electricians had attached, according to Fred Seely's instructions, water, drain, and electrical lines to each of the concrete cores. In 1955, in order to replace many of the aging lines, the stones were removed, but in modernizing the Great Hall, the decision was made not to replace them. Instead, using wood, wire, and plaster, the Merchant Construction Company turned each of the square, concrete columns into smooth, oval cylinders covered with aqua vinyl wallpaper. The granite stones, some still bearing their original mottoes, were incorporated into other parts of the building, where fragments of faded

sayings can still be seen. At the same time, the decorators convinced Leach that the stone walls flanking each of the two massive fireplaces should be covered. In front of each of the four end sections of original granite boulders, carpenters constructed a false wall covered in the same aqua vinyl wallpaper. Although the decision to cover the granite walls and pillars emphasized the fireplaces, the Great Hall lost part of its charm and character. "That was," according to Ed Leach, "our greatest mistake."

Any original wicker furniture remaining in the Great Hall in 1955 was moved to the third floor Palm Court, placed into storage, or shipped to the Jack Tar Hotel in Galveston. The oak paddle-arm furniture purchased in 1940 was refinished and re-covered; additional modern furniture filled the voids left by the removal of the wicker rockers. The original tile floor in the Great Hall was thoroughly cleaned and new rugs were laid down. A canvas awning was installed over the Sunset Terrace, which had remained uncovered since 1913. Below the south end of the terrace, Charles Sammons had the workmen construct a cloverleaf-shaped swimming pool in 1956. Newly appointed chief engineer Bill Neilson, who had worked at the Grove Park Inn since 1932, recalled that they kept the pool filled throughout the winter when the inn was closed, but floated logs in the water to keep it from freezing. Farther down the hill, the original tennis court was resurfaced, and below it, on the plateau between the two red-tiled pavilions, a Grove Park Inn landmark — a lighted fountain in the middle of a fragrant flower garden — was sacrificed for a second tennis court.

As part of their modernization program, Sammons and Leach decided to create the Dogwood cocktail lounge and restaurant on the southwest terrace overlooking the swimming pool and golf course. Glass windows were installed in what is presently the Carolina Cafe. Prior to the addition of the Sammons Wing in 1984, the cocktail lounge ran the width of the south end of the building, featuring what earlier had been an outdoor fireplace with a protective hammered-copper hood.

At the other end of the building, the inn's main dining room was also redecorated. It had originally featured two open dining areas separated by three steps, but now the floor in the lower portion was raised to place all diners on the same level. The Plantation Room, as it was called after 1955, still featured the original Roycroft lighting fixtures, but they, like nearly all of the hammered-copper fixtures in the Grove Park Inn, had mistakenly been chemically cleaned and polished. Wall-to-wall carpeting, heavy drapes with wide valances, along with new chairs, tables, china, and silverware, were added to the original dining room. Had it not been for the Roycroft lighting fixtures, the two massive sideboards, and the four corner servers, it might have looked like any modern hotel restaurant.

The new management at the Grove Park Inn made the decision to dispose of some of the original furnishings in 1956. Though this decision was later criticized, in the management's defense it must be noted that the forty-three-year-old furniture was neither old enough to be considered antique nor new enough to be considered contemporary. The now-famous "GPI" dining chairs, characterized by the three initials carved across the crestrail and the Roycroft "R" carved on the back post, were sold to the public for four dollars each. The majority of the chairs were purchased by Asheville citizens and for years afterwards could be seen on front porches around the city.

The management did keep and refinish nearly all of the original White Furniture Company bedroom suites in the 142 remaining guest rooms; only the rocking chairs were removed. Those that were not needed on the Sunset Terrace were sold. The management also made some changes to the guest rooms, beginning by removing the oak-and-burlap wall treatment on the lower six feet of the walls. This style of decorating was popular during the Arts & Crafts era (1895-1925) when the inn was designed, but by 1955 was considered outdated and unsanitary. The oak beds were also altered, first by cutting down the tall footboards and later by removing them altogether. Roycroft ceiling lights with glass globes were left intact, but any ceiling lights with solid copper bottoms were modified to accommodate either round glass globes or flat glass panels. The Roycroft desk lamps, three of which had been placed in each room, had their original copper-domed shades replaced by parchment or cloth shades.

Several of the guest rooms in the north and south wings had shared connecting bathrooms, for they had been designed by Fred Seely for families traveling with children. More important than a private bath in 1913 were two large trunk closets, required to hold clothing for an extended stay. Ed Leach proposed turning the extra closet in each room into a private bath. The management also experimented with wall-to-wall carpeting in a few of the guest rooms, but the majority of the rooms, which featured a center slab of concrete (intended to be covered by a rug) and an outer band of tile, were decorated with new rugs. As a final touch, each of the guest rooms was completely outfitted with new linens, from bedspreads and sheets to curtains and towels.

The famous Roycroft shopmark appears on many of the lighting fixtures, chairs, and sideboards still being used at the inn.

The newly renovated Grove Park Inn opened for business in April of 1956 under the direction of general manager George Stobie. Beginning that year, the Grove Park Inn became a seasonal resort, closing for the winter from November until early April. Even before the first guests arrived, including in 1956 Vice President Richard Nixon and the Reverend Billy Graham, plans were on the drafting table for a major addition. Both Charles Sammons and Ed Leach realized the inn's facilities were inadequate for conventions requiring a large number of guest rooms and meeting rooms, as well as a spacious ballroom. The era of long-term family guests had vanished, forcing hotels like the Grove Park Inn to compete for conventions in order to survive. "We recognized from the beginning that we needed to add rooms," Leach observed, "but we also knew that people were flocking to the newest rage — motels. We didn't want — and couldn't have if we tried — to turn the Grove Park Inn into a motel, but we made the decision to build Fairway Lodge next to it so that hopefully we could attract new business."

The two-story motor lodge was designed by Texas architect Thomas Price, who had assisted Sammons and Leach with the inn's remodeling plans. The site they selected was southwest of the original Main Inn, where it sat adjacent to the new swimming pool and offered guests a panoramic view of the eighteen-hole golf course. By leaving undisturbed many of the pine trees planted in 1913, Price was able to design a semi-secluded addition, while providing the modern conveniences the public demanded. Covered walkways led to the swimming pool and the Sunset Terrace, providing guests with convenient access to the restaurants and cocktail lounge. While the $200,000 Fairway Lodge provided the Grove Park Inn with an additional fifty guest rooms, convention planners also required meeting rooms and a ballroom, prompting the new management to include in its first expansion program a number of new and remodeled meeting rooms. In the original south wing, where in 1913 there had been four parlors, a writing room, and management offices — all of which had been transformed into small meeting rooms prior to World War II — the Laurel Room was created in the area presently occupied by several shops. Next to it was the Green Room, which, like the Laurel, was available for meetings, presentations, or formal banquets. An adjacent kitchen was created to service both of these rooms, plus the Dogwood Terrace, known today as the Carolina Cafe.

Although it was painted contemporary colors during the Sammons era remodeling, the Palm Court remained as it had been since 1913.

In the lower level of the Grove Park Inn, the room that had originally housed the indoor swimming pool was remodeled and named the Grotto Room. The room where guests forty years earlier had bowled and played billiards became the Cherokee Room, and the original auditor's office and Fred Seely's first office were transformed into the Mountaineer Room. All were intended to be used for meetings and convention activities. Several years later, all of these rooms in the lower level became offices for various departments of the hotel staff.

The Sammons expansion program continued into the sixties with the construction of the North Wing, which was built during the winter of 1963 and opened in April of 1964. Designed primarily to provide the Grove Park Inn with a ballroom and two more meeting rooms, the North Wing added another forty-six rooms to the inn, bringing the total number of guest rooms to 238. Unlike the Fairway Lodge, the seven-story North Wing was directly attached to the Main Inn, projecting to the west in the area presently occupied by the Vanderbilt Wing. The Plantation Room and the kitchen behind it compelled the architect to design a covered walkway leading from the Sunset Terrace to the new addition. Once inside the 5,456-square-foot ballroom, guests found nothing to indicate that the new facility was even remotely connected with the 1913 Grove Park Inn. The inspiration for the painted woodwork, elaborate crown moldings, formal drapes, blue carpeting, and polished brass lighting fixtures, described in promotional literature as "exquisitely detailed in the tradition of the Carolinas," was drawn from the Federalist era of the late eighteenth and early ninteenth centuries rather than the Arts & Crafts era of the original Main Inn.

Through the untiring efforts of general managers George Stobie, who remained at the inn from 1955 until 1964, and, later, Rushton Hays, the Grove Park Inn began the long climb back to respectability. These two general managers built a strong staff that, along with a greatly improved facility, encouraged many conventions, groups, and guests to return to the inn. In 1968, however, Charles Sammons sold six of his hotels, including the Grove Park Inn, to the Osias Resort Hotels corporation. Although the new owners announced ambitious plans for the Asheville hotel, they lacked adequate financing and strong management. Less than two years later, having done little to improve the Grove Park Inn, they defaulted on their mortgage, and Charles Sammons once again assumed ownership.

The addition of the swimming pool in 1956 helped attract the growing number of tourists vacationing in Asheville each summer.

State of North Carolina
Department of Cultural Resources
Division of Archives and History

This is to certify that

GROVE PARK INN

has been entered on

THE NATIONAL REGISTER OF HISTORIC PLACES

by the

United States Department of the Interior
upon nomination by the State Historic Preservation Officer under
provisions of the National Historic Preservation Act of 1966 (P.L. 89-665).

The National Register is a list of properties "significant in American history, architecture, archeology, and culture — a comprehensive index of the significant physical evidences of our national patrimony." Properties listed thereon deserve to be preserved by their owners as a part of the cultural heritage of our nation.

Director, Division of Archives and History
and
State Historic Preservation Officer

April 3, 1973
Date

Ed Leach had retired as president of Jack Tar Hotels in 1968 and for the next ten years the staff at the Asheville hotel watched as a series of general managers came and went in quick succession. Without consistent leadership, the Grove Park Inn, which still operated from only April until November each year, began to stagnate. In Dallas, the financial empire of Charles Sammons continued to swell, eventually branching out into commercial printing, advertising, life and health insurance, travel services, and oil drilling supplies, bottled spring water, and cable television. The Jack Tar Hotels corporation expanded as well, with an emphasis on full-service beach resorts. Increasing demands on his time and energy made it impossible for Charles Sammons to spend more than a few weeks each year at the Grove Park Inn. The initial spurt in convention business after the opening of the North Wing in 1964 soon sputtered, due primarily to the inn's limited facilities and lack of consistent internal manage-ment. Fueled by the short-lived sale of the Grove Park Inn in 1968 to the Osias corporation, rumors of an impending sale began to swirl around the hotel by the early seventies.

In 1976, Charles Sammons faced one of his most difficult decisions regard-ing the Grove Park Inn. It had become increasingly apparent that the Grove Park Inn could not evolve into a world-class resort using a borrowed golf course. More than one convention group had either vowed never to return or had spurned an invitation to meet at the Grove Park Inn because the inn did not have its own golf course. Charles Sammons recognized what Edwin W. Grove had known as early as

1909: the success or failure of the Grove Park Inn as a resort hotel would, to a large degree, be determined by the availability of a quality golf course for its guests. The members of the adjacent Country Club of Asheville owned a clubhouse, tennis courts, swimming pool, and approximately one hundred acres of land — on which Donald J. Ross in 1924 had designed one of the finest eighteen-hole golf courses in the South. Since 1913 the members had attempted to work with the inn's owners to make the course available to their guests, but the arrangement was seldom ideal for either the club or the hotel.

Although various owners of the Grove Park Inn, including Charles Sammons, had attempted to purchase the club's land and buildings, the membership, whose heritage could be traced back to the original 1893 Swannanoa Hunt Club, refused to relinquish control of the property. In 1976, however, Miami millionaire Colonel Mitchell Wolfson initiated a proposal that would affect the future of the Grove Park Inn. Wolfson, who had built a multimedia empire from a single Miami movie theatre, had spent part of nearly every summer in Asheville. Over the years he had acquired more than one hundred acres of rolling pasture around Beaver Lake, where he raised Angus cattle and thoroughbred race horses. In the early forties, he bought the bankrupt Beaver Lake golf course to prevent developers from destroying the scenic splendor of the north Asheville area. Sensing that the golf course might, after his death, be destroyed, Wolfson formulated a plan to insure its future. It soon became known around Asheville as "The Big Swap."

Fred Seely decorated the walls of the Main Inn and Biltmore Industries with motivational bits of wisdom for the benefit of guests and staff.

In essence, though negotiations consumed several months, the plan was quite simple. The Country Club of Asheville agreed to sell to the Jack Tar Hotels corporation on November 19, 1976, for approximately $2,900,000, the eighteen-hole golf course and all of the buildings, land, and facilities associated with it. The Country Club of Asheville then proceeded to purchase from Lakeview Properties, a Wolfson-owned company, the Beaver Lake golf course for approximately $1,675,000, a figure that even by conservative estimates was well below the actual

market value of the land. The profit the Country Club of Asheville generated from the sale was immediately invested in the construction of a new clubhouse and other improvements on the Beaver Lake property. Country club members were permitted to continue to use the facilities and golf course adjacent to the Grove Park Inn for the next two years, while their new building was being constructed. Then, in 1978, the facility below the inn was renamed the Grove Park Country Club.

An early drawing of the Country Club of Asheville buildings, as designed by Architect H. T. Lindeberg, and constructed in 1926.

For Charles Sammons, the decision to invest nearly three million dollars in the purchase of the country club property represented an even greater affirmation of his commitment to transform the Grove Park Inn into a world-class resort hotel. As he would soon discover, the addition of the golf course and country club facility would provide a foundation for a future expansion program that would dwarf all that he had done since 1955 for the historic inn. Missing from the formula for a successful transformation, though, was a general manager who could assist in carrying out his plans, much as Fred Seely had done for E. W. Grove.

In 1976, the clubhouse and grounds of the Country Club of Asheville became a part of the Grove Park Inn. Members were permitted to use the facility until 1978, when their new clubhouse in north Asheville was completed.

We talked to several designers until we found someone who appreciated the inn as much as we did. Mr. Sammons and I wanted them to make the new wings look as much like the old as possible by duplicating the Roycroft furniture and by using authentic antiques.

Elaine D. Sammons
May 3, 1991

RENOVATION AND EXPANSION:
1978 - 1991

Completion of the 202-room Sammons Wing in 1984 enabled the inn to return to year-round occupancy.

Gazing up at the stately Grove Park Inn from Kimberly Avenue in 1978, a casual observer might never have suspected the problems looming behind its granite walls. News of the purchase two years earlier of the Country Club of Asheville had reassured local citizens that Charles Sammons had no intention of abandoning the sixty-five-year-old hotel. But employees at the Grove Park Inn, which still operated only from April until November, had witnessed the arrival and departure of a steady stream of general managers since 1964. Serious structural problems in all three of the resort's buildings — the Main Inn, the 1958 Fairway Lodge, and the 1964 North Wing — were being either ignored or

hastily patched, rather than properly repaired. To add to the dilemma, it soon became apparent that the clubhouse adjacent to the golf course was in far worse condition than anyone had expected. Termites had so effectively weakened the walls of the picturesque clubhouse that it was feared it would have to be demolished.

Sammons, by his own admission, had had little experience in the hotel industry, and had neither the time nor the insight to recognize the quiet deterioration of his investment. Most of his general managers opted for a quiet departure once it became clear they could not deal with the mounting number of problems the hotel posed.

(Left) *The soft, graceful curves of the roof reflect the architect's appreciation for the natural skyline of the Blue Ridge Mountains.*

(Below left) *The Ann Hathaway cottage, known today as the Presidential Cottage, was built shortly after the Main Inn to the exact specifications of the English cottage where William Shakespeare's wife was born.*

(Below) *These rock-lined steps have guided guests from the Main Inn to the hillside below since 1913. Each April the dogwoods add their beauty to the natural splendor of the inn.*

(Left) *As Fred Seely described it in 1920, the Palm Court "occupying the center of the main building extends to the roof and is capped with an enormous skylight which admits an ocean of sunlight. The effect is a most delightful sun-parlor to be enjoyed on cool days, as well as a sitting-room for evenings."*

(Below) *Rooms in the Main Inn still offer guests many of the same features of seventy-five years ago: Roycroft lights, mission oak furniture, unique architectural details, and fantastic views of the Blue Ridge Mountains.*

On September 23, 1982, Charles A. Sammons, Elaine Sammons, and general manager Herman von Treskow unveiled plans for the 202-room Sammons Wing addition. (Ewart Ball, Citizen-Times)

Like his predecessor, Edwin W. Grove, with whom he shared many similarities, Charles Sammons had not been immune from personal tragedy. On a Saturday morning in 1962, his wife, Rosine, had fallen to her death in their new home. For several months afterwards, Sammons had busied himself

with projects outside of Dallas. Jack Tar Hotels owned a resort property in the Bahamas, which continued to present the owner with new challenges. Sammons had begun making regular trips to the Bahama resort, spending time in the Jack Tar sales office in Miami on his way. It was there he had renewed his acquaintance with one of

his employees, Elaine Schloff, who had worked for Jack Tar Hotels for several years before and after her husband's death. Friendship had evolved into romance and, in November of 1963, they were married.

In 1978, as yet another management change was being contemplated, Charles Sammons learned of a young man who was looking for the opportunity to manage an American hotel. Herman von Treskow, born in Posen, Germany, on April 1, 1944, had been trained in the European fashion and was a graduate of the famed Heidelberg hotel management school in Germany. Charles and Elaine Sammons believed that they had discovered a manager who could carry out their plans for the renovation of the Grove Park Inn. At the age of 34, von Treskow was ready to join them in their determined battle to rescue the inn from chronic deterioration. In October of 1978, von Treskow and his wife, Margaret, arrived at the Grove Park Inn. "We flew in here with two babies, four suitcases, and no idea what to expect," he recalled.

Charles Sammons and his new general manager faced a serious challenge. Once the pride of Asheville, the Grove Park Inn had become outdated. Sammons soon became aware of what the engineering staff at the hotel had known for years: the twenty-year-old Fairway Lodge had not been designed for winter occupancy, and the hastily constructed North Wing was already starting to develop problems. The Main Inn was in trouble, too. Far less had actually been accomplished in 1955 to solve serious plumbing and electrical problems than had been thought; what little that had been done beyond the cosmetic was already deteriorating. The electrical system was dangerously overloaded, the pipes leaked, and the heating system in the guest rooms ranged from erratic to nearly nonexistent. The inn was in dire need of a complete overhaul, and Sammons was not about to turn his back on it. He was determined to bring all of his resources to bear on the task of restoring and preserving the Grove Park Inn.

With a new general manager and the staff he assembled, Charles Sammons was confident the inn could be saved. Together he and von Treskow began making plans for the future of the Grove Park Inn. The success of his many other ventures provided the financial foundation upon which a vigorous revitalization would be built. He and his wife, Elaine, began making regular trips from their home in Dallas to Asheville. With her extensive experience in hotel management, Elaine Sammons took a special interest in the Grove Park Inn and the challenges it presented. She recognized that one of the inn's greatest assets was its heritage. Rather than attempting to disguise its age behind plaster and paint, she suggested they emphasize the historic nature of the inn. Architectural details unique to the era in which it was designed and constructed — granite walls, oak woodwork, Arts & Crafts furniture, and copper lighting fixtures — were to be preserved and duplicated throughout the Main Inn and subsequent additions. "Mr. Sammons and I loved Asheville, we loved the climate, and we knew the inn could be made even better than it was," she said, "and it was time to do it." She encouraged her husband to undertake not simply a remodeling of the Grove Park Inn, but an historic restoration designed to preserve its heritage in both the Main Inn and future additions.

(Left) *In their factory in Mebane, N.C., workmen at the White Furniture Company produced the original bedroom furniture, much of which is still being used today. The lamps shown here each bear the Roycroft shopmark.*

(Right) *The famous eight-foot Roycroft clock stood in the Great Hall from 1913 until 1984, when it was moved to a more secure location. In all likelihood, the quotation on the front of the clock, like those on the stones, was selected by Fred Seely.*

(Left) *Each of the two 36-foot-wide fireplaces in the Great Hall rises two stories and required, according to Fred Seely, "120 tons of boulders to build." The fireboxes were designed to burn eight-foot logs to warm guests on a chilly winter's eve.*

(Right) *Guests are continually amazed to learn that the two elevators constructed within the massive granite fireplaces in the Great Hall still transport guests to their rooms.*

(Below left) *In 1913 the Roycrofters produced large copper lanterns for the terraces surrounding the inn. These lanterns provided the inspiration for many of the new lights in the Vanderbilt Wing.*

(Below right) *Victor Toothaker, a Roycroft artist and metalsmith, designed several styles of lighting fixtures for the hotel, including glass-and-copper chandeliers for the guest rooms and hallways.*

Charles Sammons did what few other owners would have done by undertaking a major expansion program while at the same time restoring the Main Inn. He and Mrs. Sammons realized the inn was caught in the ambiguity of being a historic 1913 inn which was married to a 1958 motor lodge. Too small to attract conventions and too large to survive without them, the Grove Park Inn would require more than just a fresh coat of paint to survive.

Their first task was the simultaneous restoration and preservation of the Main Inn. Since purchasing the hotel, Sammons had grown more cognizant of the historical significance of the Grove Park Inn. Much had been done — and left undone — during the inn's 1955 renovation which now demanded their attention. Starting in 1978, hundreds of feet of water and electrical lines were replaced, the antiquated heating system was improved, and the famous elevators were rebuilt. The granite walls and concrete floors presented innumerable challenges to the staff and workmen who were renovating the Main Inn. The process took several months, during which time the inn remained open from April until November.

Included in the plan for the Main Inn was a bar in the Great Hall. In 1979, after lawmakers had passed a bill permitting liquor by the drink, a bar was constructed in the southwest corner to serve guests in that room and on the Sunset Terrace. But this outdoor porch presented its own problems. Guests in the rooms overlooking the Sunset Terrace would flip cigarettes out their windows, burning holes in the canvas awning. A sudden shower would send diners scurrying into the Great Hall. By the spring of 1980, though, a permanent roof designed in the same style of the inn had been constructed, giving the inn what seemed like a new room.

While the management was dedicated to the task of preserving the integrity of the historic Main Inn, it also recognized the need for a major expansion program. Once the Main Inn had been stabilized, the second step was taken in the revitalization project: expansion. In this instance, expansion had to begin with demolition.

Charles and Elaine Sammons developed a plan to transform the Grove Park Inn into a major hotel, attracting both large conventions and social guests. In order to achieve their goal, the inn would have to have approximately 500 guest rooms and a wide array of convention facilities, including additional restaurants, ballrooms, and meeting rooms. Standing in their way, however, was the twenty-one-year-old Fairway Lodge. Designed at a time when motor lodges were popular, the three-story structure no longer seemed appropriate next to the historic Main Inn. The proposal was made to demolish the Fairway Lodge and to construct in its place a 202-room addition with more than eleven thousand square feet of meeting space — all designed to complement rather than clash with the architectural style of the original Grove Park Inn. Charles Sammons listened intently as the plan was being presented, then asked, "How much is it going to cost?"

"Twenty million dollars," was the reply.

"Do it."

Construction of the Sammons Wing began in the fall of 1982. It was unveiled on April 20, 1984.

(Above) *The addition of the Sammons Wing paved the way for year-round operation of the hotel.*

(Left) *Often mistaken for the Great Smoky Mountains farther west, the Blue Ridge Mountains, as seen from the Vanderbilt Wing, surround the plateau on which Asheville is built.*

(Right) *The lobby in the Sammons Wing reveals how effectively the architects and designers blended the old with the new, drawing upon the oak woodwork and copper lighting fixtures of the Main Inn for their inspiration.*

(Below) *Architect Fred Seely's basic design for the Main Inn remains intact more than seventy-seven years later.*

On November 15, 1982, at the close of the inn's regular season, the piers beneath the twenty-four-year-old Fairway Lodge were uprooted and the two-story structure tumbled down the slope of Sunset Mountain. In a matter of hours, bulldozers had begun to clear away the remains of the ill-fated addition and were at work preparing the hillside for the foundation of the new Sammons Wing. Seventy years earlier on that same slope, Fred L. Seely, Oscar Mills, and the first construction crew built the Main Inn using teams of mules and a solitary steamshovel; the Daniel Construction Company utilized cranes and even a helicopter to assemble the nine-story addition. Rather than overshadowing the historic Main Inn, the Sammons Wing was designed as a continuation, with the undulatory curves of the red-shingled roof below the roofline of the original hotel. The top floor, which contains the Heritage Ballroom, a lounge, a restaurant, and several meeting rooms, is an extension of the Great Hall; the eight lower guest floors are built into the hillside and overlook the eighteen-hole golf course. Included in the plans for the Sammons Wing was an indoor swimming pool, for the Grove Park Inn was going to reopen as a year-round resort for the first time since the mid-fifties.

While the contractor assembled the steel skeleton of the Sammons Wing, another crew renovated the Main Inn, including the Great Hall. They tore down the oval facades around the six concrete columns, replacing plumbing and electrical lines as they progressed. The decision to recover the six columns, the north and south walls, and the front desk with oak rather than granite (which had been removed or covered in the winter of 1955) was analyzed quite carefully; in the end, it was agreed that the Great Hall could be improved by the color and texture of oak boards rather than a return to the monotony of an all-granite, all-gray interior. The small tiles in the floor had begun to break loose and disappear, so they were replaced with slabs of gray slate, duplicating the color of the original floor with a material natural to the mountain region. The same slate continued uninterrupted throughout the lobby level of the Sammons Wing. The transition from the old to the new was further accomplished by utilizing granite stones on the new interior walls. Only a close inspection will reveal where the original stonework stopped in 1913 and the new began in 1984.

Upon her arrival in 1963, Mrs. Sammons had put a stop to the former practice of discarding and selling original furnishings handcrafted by the Roycrofters and White Furniture Company. She instructed Design Continuum, their interior designers from Atlanta, to purchase authentic Arts & Crafts antiques, including Morris chairs, box settles, sideboards, and china cabinets by Gustav Stickley, Charles Limbert, and L. & J.G. Stickley, as well as quality reproductions, to fill the Great Hall and Sammons Wing lobby. The interior designers worked to maintain a harmony between the original Main Inn and the new Sammons Wing. The addition of scores of Arts & Crafts antiques created a smooth flow between the two sections. The antiques also enabled the Grove Park Inn staff to point with pride to the largest collection of authentic Arts & Crafts furniture and lighting fixtures in the entire country.

Inspecting the Sammons Wing in May of 1983 are (left to right) Herman von Treskow, Charles and Elaine Sammons, and Joe Kanewske, vice president of Sammons Enterprises.

(Left) *Portrait of Elaine D. Sammons*

(Right) *Portrait of Charles A. Sammons*

(Right) *Dogwood blossoms below the Sunset Terrace signal the arrival of spring.*

(Left) *What is presently the Carolina Cafe began as an open terrace in 1913, but was enclosed for casual dining during the fifties and named the Dogwood Terrace. The Roycroft lighting fixtures on the stone walls came from the inn's original dining room when it was remodeled in 1988.*

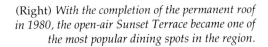

(Right) *With the completion of the permanent roof in 1980, the open-air Sunset Terrace became one of the most popular dining spots in the region.*

(Below) *Despite many changes, the Great Hall is still the heart of the inn. During the 1984 renovation, antique Morris chairs were added to the inn's Arts & Crafts collection, making it one of the largest in the country.*

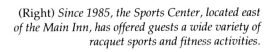

(Right) *Since 1985, the Sports Center, located east of the Main Inn, has offered guests a wide variety of racquet sports and fitness activities.*

But the crowning glory of the new Sammons Wing was the 8,778-square-foot Heritage Ballroom. Elegant, yet functional, the Heritage Ballroom, like the entire Sammons Wing, was designed and decorated to complement, not compete with, the Main Inn. Oak woodwork, carefully selected draperies and carpets, and custom-designed copper chandeliers handcrafted in the Arts & Crafts style provided the perfect backdrop for the delicate balance of authentic antiques and accurate reproductions. The Heritage Ballroom could seat one thousand diners and its carefully planned and positioned kitchen could also service the inn's most elegant new restaurant. When, on April 20, 1984, the newly renovated and expanded Grove Park Inn opened its doors for year-round occupancy, it had much to offer: 410 rooms, four restaurants, two lounges, two ballrooms, expanded convention facilities, and something no amount of money could construct — a proud history.

History repeats itself: in the spring of 1984, as stonemasons complete the final wall outside the Sammons Wing, general manager Herman von Treskow uses a wagon and team of horses to haul the final load of boulders for the new addition. To the right of von Treskow is Jimmie Stepp, owner of Stepp's Stone Works.

For the owners and management of the Grove Park Inn, the restoration of the Main Inn and the completion of the Sammons Wing signaled the beginning of the third phase of their plan: the renovation of the country club facility. Increased business from regional and national corporate conventions, as well as vacationers in the Blue Ridge Mountains, would create additional demands on the hotel's golf course and clubhouse. The rambling, Norman-style clubhouse, built in 1926, had badly deteriorated; what began as a remodeling project quickly evolved into an extensive restoration, as workmen discovered termite damage throughout the entire structure. Once again, Charles Sammons provided the financial support — more than one million dollars — to renovate the clubhouse, restaurant, outdoor swimming pool, and golf course. When it reopened on June 11, 1985, the Grove Park Inn could point with pride to one of the finest country club facilities in the entire state.

Yet even before the country club renovation was complete, a new structure was being built on the hotel grounds. Little more than one hundred yards east of the Main Inn, across from the original site of Sunset Hall, the 32,514-square-foot Sports Center was being constructed. This completely separate facility opened on December 22, 1985, giving guests that winter the opportunity to enjoy two racquetball courts, three tennis courts, a squash court, a weight training room, an aerobics room, whirlpools, and saunas.

Although the addition of the golf course, the Grove Park Country Club, the Sports Center, and the Sammons Wing had transformed the hotel into a full-service resort and conference center, Charles and Elaine Sammons remained dedicated to the attainment of their goal of a 500-room resort.

On December 15, 1986, detonation charges carefully placed around the foundation of the North Wing neatly dropped the seven-story structure at the foot of the inn without damage to the seventy-three-year-old granite walls. Once again, bulldozers and construction crews descended on the site, paving the way for the final phase of the Grove Park Inn's expansion.

Drawing their inspiration from both the Main Inn and the Sammons addition, the architects and interior designers of the 413,250-square-foot Vanderbilt Wing gracefully blended the old with the new. Once again, the soft roof lines reflected those of the Main Inn and remained below the original red-tiled roof. The Vanderbilt Wing connector was designed to display antiques, documents and photographs from the inn's past. The walkway to the Blue Ridge Dining Room was paved with gray slate and decorated with Arts & Crafts antiques, accurate reproductions, and hammered-copper lighting fixtures.

(Below) *The old and the new: the original Roycroft sideboards and lighting fixtures designed in 1913 are combined with a new version of the "GPI" chair in the Blue Ridge Dining Room.*

(Bottom, from left to right) *One of the most secluded spots at the inn is the courtyard outside Elaine's nightclub in the Vanderbilt Wing.*

Among the antiques purchased for the inn since 1984 are these Roycroft chairs, a Lifetime sideboard, and a photograph of Elbert Hubbard (1856-1915), who founded the Roycroft Shops in East Aurora, New York.

One of the original Roycroft GPI chairs and a china cabinet by L. & J.G. Stickley are displayed in the memorabilia exhibit in the Vanderbilt Wing connector. The exhibit is part of the Grove Park Inn Archives, dedicated to preserving the history of the inn and its many famous guests.

This rare, six-foot Roycroft clock was originally commissioned for Fred Seely. For years it remained in one of the inn's suites, until it was placed on display in the memorabilia exhibit.

*The parlor suites in the Vanderbilt Wing offer a rare
combination of elegance, space, and breathtaking
views of the Blue Ridge Mountains.*

Located more than one hundred feet above the ground, the Blue Ridge Dining Room provides guests with panoramic views of the Asheville skyline and distant mountains. The addition of this four-hundred-seat restaurant changed the role of the original Grove Park Inn dining room. After carefully removing the original Roycroft chandeliers, wall sconces, and massive oak buffets for installation in the new Blue Ridge Dining Room, workmen remodeled the Plantation Room into staff offices. Though over the course of seventy-five years, it had served five Presidents and scores of dignitaries, the Plantation Room was too small and its kitchen too outdated to make the transition from serving three hundred guests to an anticipated one thousand diners.

Two hundred fifty pounds of explosives were detonated in a series of eight timed charges designed to "implode" the North Wing on December 15, 1986. In the first photograph, the initial charges have shattered the internal piers, causing the outer walls to buckle. In the second photograph, the upper seven floors collapse in controlled sequence. A few seconds later the wing has been reduced to a pile of rubble. Workmen can be seen spraying water to minimize the dust filtering into the Main Inn. (Photographs by J. Weiland)

Although the eleven-story Vanderbilt Wing did provide the Grove Park Inn with 166 new guest rooms, most, like those in the Sammons Wing, furnished with reproduction Arts & Crafts oak furniture, its primary purpose was to give the inn convention facilities that would rival or surpass any in the Southeast. To complement the 8,778-square-foot Heritage Ballroom in the Sammons Wing, the Grand Ballroom, on the eighth floor in the Vanderbilt addition, offered 17,676 square feet of convention hall space capable of seating nearly two thousand people. With the official opening of the Vanderbilt Wing and the completion of the expansion program, the Grove Park Inn's statistics were impressive: 140 acres of grounds, 510 guest rooms, four restaurants, three lounges, two ballrooms, forty meeting rooms, a country club and eighteen-hole golf course, two swimming pools, indoor and outdoor sports facilities, more than six hundred employees, and an annual payroll in excess of ten million dollars. And located in the center of it all is the jewel of the Grove Park Inn crown – the historic Main Inn.

Bulldozers carved out the hillside in the spring of 1987 to prepare for the construction of the Vanderbilt Wing, which opened on August 19, 1988, increasing the number of rooms in the hotel to 510. (Dan Maxheimer, Citizen-Times)

(Left) *The open staircase and glass elevator in the Vanderbilt Wing give guests an opportunity to view the exterior wall of the original Main Inn, now an interior wall in the Atrium Lobby.*

(Right) *The indoor swimming pool in the Sammons Wing is adjacent to the children's activity room and the tiled terrace, often used for sunbathing.*

On September 7, 1988, Elaine Sammons and Herman von Treskow placed a time capsule in the cornerstone of the newly completed Vanderbilt Wing. Scheduled to be opened on the hotel's 100th anniversary, the capsule contains a variety of inn memorabilia. Shown on the left is Maggie Schlubach, director of public relations.

Today, the Grove Park Inn has become a four-season resort, highlighted by numerous annual events. One of their most famous, A Grove Park Inn Christmas, runs the entire month of December, when the inn is lavishly decorated and features special seasonal exhibits. Other annual events include All That Jazz, the Comedy Classic, the Heritage Ballroom Dance Classic, the national Arts & Crafts Conference and Antiques Show, and several other theme weekends.

Charles A. Sammons died at the age of ninety on November 12, 1988, less than three months after the opening of the Vanderbilt Wing and the successful completion of the ambitious sixty-five million dollar expansion and renovation program which he had financed. Although his empire was estimated to be worth in excess of two billion dollars, he had remained throughout his life a shy, quiet man, content to give those who worked in his organization the opportunity to manage his businesses as if they were their own. Though he maintained his home in Dallas, where he gave generously to numerous charitable organizations, particularly in medicine and the arts, he and his wife, Elaine, had continued to visit North Carolina on a regular basis, for they, like many others, maintained "a love affair with Asheville" — and the Grove Park Inn.

The death of Charles A. Sammons in 1988 marked the end of an era of tremendous expansion for the seventy-five-year-old Grove Park Inn. Three years later, on June 12, 1991, general manager Herman von Treskow left his post after nearly thirteen years at the inn. Without Edwin Grove in 1912, the inn might never have been built. Without Charles Sammons in 1955, it might never have been saved. These two men, their capable general managers, Fred L. Seely and Herman von Treskow, and the thousands of people who have worked at the Grove Park Inn since the first shovelful of dirt was turned on July 9, 1912, have made it possible for countless numbers of guests to breathe the clean air, to walk amid tall pines, to warm themselves before a blazing hearth, and to take home treasured memories of a journey to the Grove Park Inn.

William Jennings Bryan, one of her first and most faithful guests, stood before a crowded room of admirers on that famous Saturday evening, July 12, 1913, to share his vision of the future of the Grove Park Inn:

I have never seen any structure to equal this. I have looked through it and marvelled at the triumph of the builder's art, and, as I gazed, the thought impressed me that these men are not building for this generation or this century, but for the age. It will stand forever. Why should not this hotel stand for all time, for it has none of the elements of decay? It will be here as an eloquent monument to its founders in the centuries to come. It was built not for the dead, as were the tombs of kings, but for living human beings that they might find delight here. Today we stand in this wonderful hotel, not built for a few, but for the multitudes that will come and go. I congratulate these men. They have built for the ages.

(Above) *At Christmas, the Grove Park Inn becomes a winter wonderland, highlighted by weekday singalongs with the staff chorus.*

(Left) *The Kimberly Avenue view of the inn, with the Vanderbilt Wing (1988) on the left, the Sammons Wing (1984) on the right, and the Main Inn (1913) in the center.*

(Right) *At the end of the Sammons Wing can be found one of the inn's formal dining rooms – the Horizons Restaurant.*

(Left) *The interior designers worked carefully to achieve a balance of antiques and accurate reproductions in the halls of the Vanderbilt Wing.*

(Right) *The open staircase in the Vanderbilt Wing provides an unusual view of the Atrium Lobby, surrounding the small pool and fountain in Elaine's Courtyard.*